The Management of Consumer Co-operatives in Korea

This book explores and analyzes cooperative management and provides insight into how Korea's consumer cooperatives have evolved and been managed. It focuses on Korea's consumer cooperative management practices and examines their growth and performance. This book is an invaluable resource for those interested to learn more about the successes and failures of consumer cooperatives.

Seungkwon Jang is Chair of Department of Management of Cooperatives at the Graduate School of Sungkonghoe University, Korea, a position he has held since 2010. He is the author of books and research articles on cooperative management and organization theory. His other research interests include fair trade value chain management and social economy organizations including social cooperatives.

Routledge Frontiers of Business Management

Gender and Family Entrepreneurship
Edited by Vanessa Ratten, Veland Ramadani, Leo-Paul Dana, Robert Hisrich and João J. Ferreira

Human Resource Management and the Global Financial Crisis
Evidence from India's IT/BPO Industry
Ashish Malik

Women Entrepreneurship in Family Business
Edited by Vanessa Ratten, Leo-Paul Dana and Veland Ramadani

Innovation and Internationalisation
Successful SMEs' Ventures into China
Stuart Orr, Jane Menzies, Connie Zheng and Sajeewa 'Pat' Maddumage

Technological Substitution in Asia
Ewa Lechman

China and Global Value Chains
Globalization and the Information and Communications Technology Sector
Yutao Sun and Seamus Grimes

Transformational Entrepreneurship
Edited by Vanessa Ratten and Paul Jones

Labor Relations and Human Resource Management in China
Connie Zheng

The Management of Consumer Co-operatives in Korea
Identity, Participation and Sustainability
Edited by Seungkwon Jang

For more information about this series, please visit www.routledge.com/Routledge-Frontiers-of-Business-Management/book-series/RFBM

The Management of Consumer Co-operatives in Korea

Identity, Participation and Sustainability

Edited by Seungkwon Jang

Routledge
Taylor & Francis Group

LONDON AND NEW YORK

First published 2020
by Routledge
2 Park Square, Milton Park, Abingdon, Oxon OX14 4RN

and by Routledge
605 Third Avenue, New York, NY 10017

First issued in paperback 2021

Routledge is an imprint of the Taylor & Francis Group, an informa business

Publisher's Note
The publisher has gone to great lengths to ensure the quality of this reprint but points out that some imperfections in the original copies may be apparent.

British Library Cataloguing-in-Publication Data
A catalogue record for this book is available from the British Library

Library of Congress Cataloging-in-Publication Data
Names: Jang, Seungkwon, editor.
Title: The management of consumer co-operatives in Korea : identity,
    participation and sustainability / edited by Seungkwon Jang.
Description: First Edition. | New York : Routledge, 2019. | Series:
    Routledge frontiers of business management | Includes bibliographical
    references and index.
Identifiers: LCCN 2019014881 | ISBN 9781138489943 (hardback) |
    ISBN 9781351036467 (ebook)
Subjects: LCSH: Consumer cooperatives—Korea (South)—Management. |
    Business logistics—Korea (South)
Classification: LCC HD3388.A4 M36 2019 | DDC 334/.5068—dc23
LC record available at https://lccn.loc.gov/2019014881

Typeset in Galliard
by Apex CoVantage, LLC

ISBN 13: 978-1-03-209182-2 (pbk)
ISBN 13: 978-1-138-48994-3 (hbk)

Contents

Figures

Tables

Contributors

Young-Jeong Cho is a doctoral student of the Department of Management of Cooperatives at the Graduate School of Sungkonghoe University, Seoul, Korea.

Woosuk Choi is Professor of the Department of Management of Cooperatives at the Graduate School of Sungkonghoe University, Seoul, Korea.

Seungkwon Jang is Professor and Head of the Department of Management of Cooperatives at the Graduate School of Sungkonghoe University, Seoul, Korea.

Jihyun Jeong is a master's student of the Department of Management of Cooperatives at the Graduate School of Sungkonghoe University, Seoul, Korea.

Minjin Ji Researcher of iCOOP Cooperative Institute, Seoul, Korea.

Sunyoung Jung is a doctoral student of the Department of Management of Cooperatives at the Graduate School of Sungkonghoe University, Seoul, Korea.

Ah Young Kim is Chairperson of iCOOP Consumer Activities, Seoul, Korea.

Dasom Kim is Assistant Manager of the Cooperatives Division at the Korea Social Enterprise Promotion Agency, Korea.

Sanghoon Lee is Professor of the Department of Management of Cooperatives at the Graduate School of Sungkonghoe University, Seoul, Korea.

Bo Young Oh is Researcher of the COOPY Cooperative, Seoul, Korea.

Sangsun Park is Associate Professor of the Department of Management of Cooperatives at the Graduate School of Sungkonghoe University, Seoul, Korea.

Jin-Seon Seo is a lecturer of the Department of Management of Cooperatives at the Graduate School, Sungkonghoe University, Seoul, Korea.

Sukhee Youn is a doctoral student of the Department of Management of Cooperatives at the Graduate School of Sungkonghoe University, Seoul, Korea.

1 Introduction

Korea's consumer cooperatives

Seungkwon Jang

Past and present of Korea's major consumer cooperatives

Consumer cooperatives in Korea have progressed slowly but steadily over the last three decades. Hansalim consumer cooperatives[1] celebrated their 30th anniversary in 2016, and Happycoop consumer cooperatives[2] were established in 1989. Dure consumer cooperatives[3] and iCOOP consumer cooperatives[4] turned 20 years old in 2017. As they have grown, consumer cooperatives have become more influential and important in Korean society in general.

It is estimated that the number of members of the four major cooperative federations is around 1.195 million households in 2018 (see Table 1.1). The number of members in 2018 accounted for 5% of that of total households in Korea, 19.56 million. Roughly 10,000 workers are employed by these four consumer cooperative federations, and 10,000 or more agricultural producers as farmer members are in business partnerships. Sales of the four major consumer cooperatives are 1,140 billion Korean won, which is equal to 1 billion US dollars (see Table 1.2). One of the main businesses of consumer cooperatives in Korea is to supply their members with organic foods, livestock, seafood, and other goods.

In this introductory chapter, a brief history and current status of Korean consumer cooperatives are illustrated. The four major consumer cooperatives in Korea have their own unique histories, philosophies, founding leaders, and members. Noticeably, the major consumer cooperatives have been developed along with their own roots of a social movement, as shown in Figure 1.1 (Jeong et al., 2011). Furthermore, the challenges of cooperatives, specifically business-related themes such as governance, finance, performance, organization, marketing, and supply chain, are discussed in terms of business and social movement.

1. Hansalim

In 1986, a humble grain store called 'Hansalim Nongsan' was opened in Seoul, where the former president and farmers sell organic rice, grains, sesame oil, and eggs (Kim, 2017). They dreamed of the world in which urban and rural

Table 1.1 The number of members in Korea's consumer cooperatives

	1998	1999	2000	2001	2002	2003	2004	2005	2006	2007	2008	2009	2010	2011	2012	2013	2014	2015	2016	2017	2018
Hansalim	22,208	26,551	31,511	41,031	60,363	76,536	99,761	115,851	132,787	147,339	170,793	207,503	247,072	293,442	346,500	410,211	481,105	535,518	596,240	643,677	661,143
Happycoop	3,025	3,444	4,186	5,351	7,745	9,532	11,155	12,077	12,911	14,457	17,187	19,579	24,900	22,795	27,280	30,170	34,435	37,615	38,224	38,473	38,316
Dure		3,000	7,891	9,665	11,651	15,907	29,856	34,627	37,670	37,157	44,575	66,617	84,712	103,874	120,000	142,359	159,593	176,138	189,370	201,964	213,168
iCOOP	663	1,229	2,470	3,330	7,538	11,645	15,368	15,368	20,097	22,350	54,660	56,100	118,824	129,666	170,127	194,856	218,585	237,610	250,980	262,507	282,720

The number of members

— iCOOP   –●– HappyCoop   ·····●····· Hansalim   –●– Dure

Table 1.2 Turnover of Korea's consumer cooperatives (year, million US$)

	1998	1999	2000	2001	2002	2003	2004	2005	2006	2007	2008	2009	2010	2011	2012	2013	2014	2015	2016	2017	2018
Hansalim	$10.6	$13.7	$16.8	$24.7	$34.4	$45.0	$63.8	$73.5	$85.1	$99.1	$120.55	$144.9	$173.5	$202.3	$230.3	$276.8	$312.5	$329.1	$355.9	$384.8	$391.3
Happycoop	$1.1	$1.5	$2.0	$2.7	$4.5	$5.2	$6.0	$6.0	$6.8	$7.8	$10.32	$14.0	$15.4	$15.5	$15.2	$15.4	$20.2	$19.1	$19.3	$19.1	$17.9
Dure	$-	$1.4	$3.5	$4.7	$7.5	$10.1	$22.7	$25.6	$28.8	$27.5	$33.45	$50.5	$63.9	$67.1	$84.4	$92.4	$100.0	$105.6	$107.5	$109.8	$111.2
iCOOP	$1.8	$2.7	$4.5	$7.3	$15.5	$26.4	$44.5	$54.5	$69.1	$85.5	$118.18	$187.3	$219.1	$272.7	$313.6	$389.1	$439.1	$478.2	$501.8	$503.6	$519.1

Yearly turnover

iCOOP · HappyCoop · Hansalim · Dure

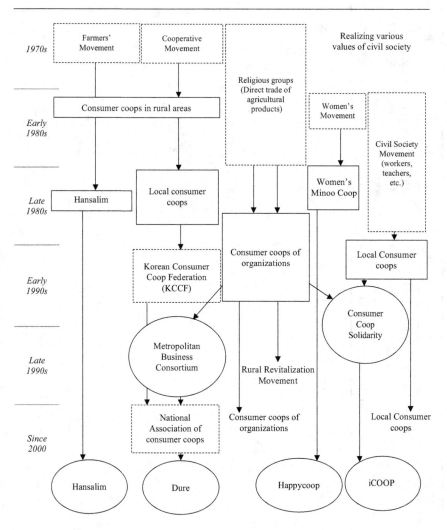

Figure 1.1 Development of Korea's consumer cooperatives.

Source: Jeong et al. (2011, p. 18, revised).

Note: Circles = coop federations, boxes = primary consumer coop, boxes with dotted lines = movements and federations, arrows = influence.

communities overcome the existing market system and live together through direct trade of eco-friendly agricultural products (Hansalim Federation, 2015). For local producers to lead the *Hansalim* Movement (literal meaning is 'save all living things'), Hansalim Producers' Association was established in 1988 (Hansalim website). During a similar period, consumers in urban areas also organized a cooperative, 'Hansalim community consumer's cooperative' (Hansalim, 2018). Through this organization, consumer members have regularly visited the producing area and built trust with producers (Hansalim website). Hansalim spread their view by announcing the Hansalim Manifesto in 1989 and inspired several social movements. Also, they contributed to organic agriculture in Korean society as taking the lead on establishing the Korean Federation of Sustainable Agriculture Organizations (Hansalim website).

In 2002, Hansalim Seoul reconstructed its organization by separating local groups, registering a corporation, establishing 'Moshim and Salim Research Institute', and organizing Hansalim Business Association around the metropolitan area (Hansalim website; Hansalim Federation, 2015). Along with the consumer movement, they started to consider a new organic certification system other than the current system. At the same time, they have raised funds for agriculture and established the solar power stations for preserving the environment (Hansalim Federation, 2015).

In 2011, Hansalim Producer Meeting, which was established in 2003, changed its name to Hansalim Federation, and it represents all the businesses and activities of Hansalim since then (Hansalim Federation, 2015; Hansalim website). Furthermore, a new distribution center has been built in 2012 where there are food-processing factories and facilities for recycling bottles (Hansalim website). Starting from a small rice shop run by only a few farmers, Hansalim consists of about 114 farmers communities and more than 661,000 households as members, and has 221 local stores nationwide in 2018 (Hansalim, 2018).

2. *Happycoop*

Happycoop consumer cooperatives (hereafter Happycoop,[5] *Hangbok Jungsim Saenghyup*) was established in 1989 with the aim to enhance gender equality and women's rights in the practice of a consumer cooperative movement organized by Women's Link (Huh, 2008). Leading Korean feminist movement Women's Link expected that the cooperation of housewives (women) would contribute not only to environmental-friendly foods but also widely to gender, education, local, and consumption issues (Kim et al., 2012: 321). In the early 1990s, despite the increasing interest in food safety issues, Happycoop showed little development (Park, 2007). The slow progress led them to set up their own vision and business plan as a consumer cooperative, hence separating them as an independent organization from Women's Link.

In 2000, they held an inaugural meeting to announce their legal corporate entity, based on the Consumer Cooperatives Act (Park, 2007; Huh, 2008). The following year, Happycoop initiated a joint logistic center and engaged discussion among primary cooperatives to increase member participation and achieve business sustainability (Park, 2007). As part of its active movement, they engage in principal associative activities, including a monthly forum, Asian Sisterhood International Meeting, and exchange meeting of women consumers and producers (Happycoop website). To ensure their business sustainability, in

2006, Happycoop adopted the slogan *Hangbok Jungsim* (Center of Happiness) and became actively engaged in social issues such as the decline of agriculture, the emergence of aging society, and women labor in a local community. In the same year, Happycoop launched three independent primary cooperatives in the Seoul metropolitan area, where each local branch manages its own retail stores (Park, 2007). Individual primary cooperatives are governed autonomously by their own board of directors and secretariat.

Then, in 2011, according to the revised Consumer Cooperatives Act, Happycoop established the Korean Federation of Women Link Cooperative (hereafter KFWL), which allows them to organize and support the primary cooperatives. Afterward, KFLS has to change the fundamental identity of women's cooperatives merging the various cooperatives and expanding the business field. Celebrating the 20th anniversary in 2013, KFWL has changed its name to Happycoop (Kim, 2012). Currently, Happycoop is developing its vision for women, local community, welfare system, alternative economy, and environmental-friendly agricultural products.[6]

3.   Dure

Dure Consumer Cooperatives' Union (hereafter Dure) as a formal organization was derived from the Korean Consumer Cooperative Federation (KCCF), whose main aim was direct trading of agricultural products to guarantee small and poor farmers and fishermen stable income, to suggest a turning point of consumer cooperatives in Korea (Jeong, 2011; Kim, 2017; Dure Consumer Cooperatives' Union, 2017). Also, it has been found due to the financial difficulties that two-thirds of consumer cooperatives in KCCF had faced during the economic crisis in 1997 (Kim, 2017). In the same year, seven main local cooperatives in Seoul metropolitan areas established the Capital Metropolitan Business Consortium to enhance the business-wise capabilities of the organizations, with financial support from Japan's consumer cooperatives such as Green Co-op, Pal system Consumer Co-operative Union, Co-op Kobe, Life Club, and so on (Dure Consumer Cooperatives' Union, 2017). They emphasized the importance of forming a sustainable and efficient distribution system for both producers and consumers, and developed a computerization program of one order per week to adjust the balance between supply and demand.

In 1999, they changed its name into the Capital Metropolitan Cooperative Association to transcend the business boundary and include all the activities and solidarity of member cooperatives (Dure Consumer Cooperatives' Union, 2017). In the meantime, the financial support from Green Co-op in Japan during the establishment of the Consortium initiated an official fund for mutual benefit between Korea and Japan in 2000 to sustain their relationship (Dure Consumer Cooperatives' Union, 2017).

Farmers who supplied agricultural products to the Consortium in the early 1990s were from various areas and not formally grouped as an organization. Since 2003, however, the Association started to recognize the needs of a formal organization for producers. This has led to the establishment of the Dure Producers Association consisting of 70 to 80 farmers (Dure Consumer Cooperatives' Union, 2017). As the organization grew, Dure again expanded its local boundary by changing its name to the Dure Consumer Cooperative Union in 2005. At 20 years old, Dure practiced cooperation with other social economy organizations, notably, creating People's Fair Trade Cooperative (PTCoop) with other consumer cooperatives for Fair Trade business that they have been doing since 2004 (PTCoop website). Dure now has a mission to enrich people's lives and recover local communities through organic farming and cooperation (Dure website).

4. *iCOOP*

The history of iCOOP consumer cooperatives (hereafter, iCOOP) traces back to 1997 when small- and medium-sized local cooperatives founded a consumer cooperatives federation (Jeong, 2011; Kim, 2017).[7] Their primary concern was to overcome the financial difficulty in direct trade of environmental-friendly agricultural products (Kim, 2017; Yeom, 2018). To reduce the high logistics costs, they integrated the logistics of each primary cooperative and implemented a membership due system (Yeom, 2018). In the early 2000s, there had been several incidents of organic food adulteration. These were happened by greedy producers, as cheap non-organic foodstuffs were mixed with high-priced authentic organic foods (Jang et al., 2004). A series of incidents made consumer cooperatives in Korea, including iCOOP, unreliable and untrustworthy as organic food providers for Korean consumers (Jang et al., 2011).

From the experience, iCOOP has set out their plans for food safety system: control, product, and production. Firstly, they have established the iCOOP certification center to ensure qualified eco-friendly agricultural products for members. In addition, they launched the retail store brand 'Natural Dream' to expand membership, ultimately to achieve economies of scale in production. Most importantly, in late 2007, they concluded an agreement to establish an eco-friendly organic food cluster in Goesan for a sustainable production and consumption base (iCOOP Union, 2018). Accordingly, iCOOP strengthened its relationships with producers by creating the Price Stabilization Fund and the Production Stabilization Fund. In response to executing new policies, iCOOP announced their identity as that of ethical consumerism and confirmed their name as *iCOOP Saenghyup*[8] (iCOOP Consumer Cooperatives). The identity implies the impact of ethical consumption on its members, the general public, and planet earth.

Besides, in 2010, based on the revised Consumer Cooperatives Act, they established the iCOOP business union of consumer cooperatives and iCOOP consumer activities, which consist of primary cooperatives to focus on their own fields of interest. Finally, iCOOP has been constructing its organic food production clusters in Gurye and Goesan. Recently, in the opening ceremony at Goesan, iCOOP celebrated its 20th anniversary and announced its future plan (iCOOP website). To achieve this, they declared new collaboration network

SAPENet for dynamic relations, not limited to consumers, farmers, and cluster partner firms, but also with the various social economy actors and NPOs to draw their potential (iCOOP, 2018).

Korea's consumer cooperatives and the ICA's Blueprint

Even if their business outcomes show significant figures, it is crucial to deal with 'cooperative management' when evaluating the performance of consumer cooperatives. There have been many failures in consumer cooperatives in Western countries, including Britain where the business model of the consumer cooperative had been invented and thrived once. Some critics are pointing out mismanagement of consumer cooperatives in their business failures. Thus, the present book focuses on describing vividly Korea's consumer cooperative management practices and investigating theoretically growth, performance, and democratic management of consumer cooperatives in Korea.

As the ICA has suggested the 'strategy for a global cooperative future' in the *Blueprint for a Co-operative Decade* published in January 2013, the global cooperative movement and businesses have been working together in learning and sharing their knowledge and practices with other cooperatives globally. Korean consumer cooperatives have learned the principles and the best practices of the global leading consumer cooperatives (noticeably, Japan's consumer cooperatives), and have shared their own successes and failures with other cooperatives locally.

According to the *Blueprint for Cooperative Decade* (International Co-operative Alliance, 2013), there are five key themes – namely, participation, sustainability, identity, capital, and legal framework. Korean consumer cooperatives are well aware of the significances of these themes for their future prosperity. This book is going to employ the same perspective of the Blueprint strategy, so the five themes are crucial for discussing the challenges and solutions Korean consumer cooperatives have faced.

The present book addresses the increasing needs for understanding Korea's cooperatives and consumer cooperatives. There are two distinctive features of this book. Firstly, most studies on cooperatives in Korea that have been published in English put their focus on Nonghyup, the Korean agricultural cooperative. In contrast, there is a lack of research on Korea's consumer cooperatives. Therefore, it provides a chance to compare and to illuminate the business dynamics of Korean cooperatives.

Secondly, the present book consists of seven research articles that explore and analyze cooperative management, including governance, marketing, finance, supply chain management, and performance of consumer cooperatives in Korea. There is a growing tendency for global cooperative researchers to conduct research on connections between management strategy, practices and performance. In addition, studies on failed cooperatives and specifically consumer cooperatives generally show that management, governance, and performance are related to each other. Therefore, the present book will be beneficial for the global audiences who are interested in the successes and failures of consumer cooperatives and especially in learning more about the management, governance, and performance of Korean consumer cooperatives.

All chapters of the present book are written by the members of the Department of Management of Cooperatives in Sungkonghoe University, one of the higher education institutions in Korea that have been training cooperative management researchers since 2010. The data and research-related materials and assistance have come from iCOOP, Hansalim, and other major consumer cooperatives and their members.

Overview of the chapters

Chapter 2[9] is concerned with 'cooperative governance' (Ah Young Kim, Young-Jeong Cho, Seungkwon Jang). The aim of the chapter is to investigate cooperative governance practice, which is the process of building consensus among various stakeholders to achieve the dual purposes of cooperatives (i.e. economic and social value creation). Weick's (1995) sensemaking theory provides a valuable perspective for cooperative generative governance. *Sensemaking* is the ability to create shared meanings of given situations and issues within an organization. It compels members to adapt themselves to everchanging environments and to achieve their organization's own goals. The present research is an exploratory case study of iCOOP, which investigates cooperative governance practice, particularly BOD's attempt to turn a crisis into an opportunity. In conclusion, cooperatives practice generative governance is the process of sensemaking with active communication.

Chapter 3[10] addresses the 'gender perspectives' for consumer cooperatives (Ah Young Kim and Seungkwon Jang). As the members of Korea's consumer cooperatives have been increasing, women are actively engaged in cooperative movement and enterprises at the same rate. However, this situation is not enough to elaborate on the female-dominant consumer cooperative landscape of Korea. According to conventional wisdom, the gender issue in Korea is male-dominant organizational culture, regenerating patriarchal organizations. This chapter provides a theoretical explanation of Korea's female-dominant cooperatives, as well as practical suggestions for a better cooperative enterprise. The knowledge creation processes in management and organization theories are reviewed by multi-faceted gender perspectives. Finally, the alternative understandings of women-dominant consumer cooperatives in Korea are discussed.

Chapter 4[11] highlights the 'price stability' in consumer cooperatives (Minjin Ji and Woosuk Choi). This chapter is based on the empirical study employing error correction model, which investigates whether the pricing system in consumer cooperatives mitigates the degree of asymmetric price transmission, and examines how consumer cooperatives could protect the consumers' welfare from the imperfect market competition. We find that the asymmetry of price transmission in a conventional agricultural products market is considerably alleviated in the pricing system of consumer cooperatives. The findings implicate that consumer cooperatives could promote a more balanced redistribution of wealth, enhancing the welfare of producers as well as consumers, and suggest the economic role of consumer cooperatives, especially in terms of the consumers' welfare.

Chapter 5 is on 'financing' consumer cooperatives (Jin-Seon Seo and Woosuk Choi). This chapter aims to explain the reason why consumer cooperatives are difficult to finance, to identify necessity of member participation in funding on the basis of financial theory, and to study some issues on the financing of consumer cooperatives. The previous research focuses mainly on the ownership of them. This chapter proposes that the reason why cooperatives have difficulty in funding capital is attributed to information asymmetry between investors and cooperatives, not to the ownership. Consumer cooperatives have insufficient ways to communicate with investors, and this may cause under-investment compared to investor-owned businesses. However, a member of the consumer cooperative is not only a consumer but also an owner, so that it is very important to communicate with members in decision-making. Conclusively, we can maintain consumer cooperatives prefer 'member loans' as a way of financing because information asymmetry with members is smaller than with others. This is consistent with 'pecking order theory'.

Chapter 6[12] explores 'brand identity' of consumer cooperatives (Sukhee Youn, Sanghoon Lee). There are four major consumer cooperatives in Korea (namely, Hansalim, iCOOP, Dure, and Happycoop), which originate from the civil movement during the 1980s. The research question is whether each cooperative's brand identity rooted in different founding ideas is still effective, even when their membership has increased, and eco-friendly food retailers other than consumer cooperatives have increased rapidly. Brand identities not only play the role of identification but also represent their core values and principles as cooperative associations. Thus, building and managing brand identities are necessary for cooperatives to establish a management strategy and future direction. The purposes of this chapter are to identify whether the brand identity each cooperative suggests having any differentiation from each other, and what it is and how its members perceive it. The chapter shows how each brand is positioned in the consumer's mind. Qualitative analysis is conducted through the documents such as annual report, publications, press releases, and in-depth interviews with CEOs to find out what brand identity each cooperative seeks to accomplish. The chapter explores what brand identity of each cooperative suggests and how its members perceive each brand.

Chapter 7[13] discusses the 'member participation' and productivity changes (Sunyoung Jung and Woosuk Choi). There are two mainstream theories of the firm. The first is contract-perspective theories, which insist firms exist to minimize the 'transaction costs' caused by asymmetric information. The second is competence-perspective theories, which assert firms subsist to develop their 'productive capabilities'. Although both theories pursue management efficiency, they disregard the social nature of firms called 'cooperation' based on trust, participation, and loyalty. In this context, this chapter aims to investigate the relationship that the participation of members and changes in productivity of consumer cooperatives using the Malmquist output-based productivity index. The analysis targeted the seven branches of Hansalim and was conducted for five years from 2012 to 2016. The data consist of annual input and output variables such as financial performance, non-financial performance, and sustainability performance. The authors calculated the Malmquist output-based productivity index for each of the seven branches in our sample. The results show that the seven branches improved their average annual productivity of 0.6% from 2012 to 2016 and only two branches had a negative change in productivity. By comparing annual changes in the productivity of seven branches, the most influential changes to productivity turned out to be technical change. This chapter shows that consumer cooperatives are a useful business form in achieving management performance and that member participation could be a prerequisite factor for positive productivity change.

Chapter 8[14] is concerned with 'supply chain management' (Dasom Kim, Sangsun Park, Seungkwon Jang). SCM (supply chain management) is an essential function of business management in either cooperative enterprises or any enterprises. It is deeply connected with value creation activities of modern enterprises so as to obtain a competitive advantage. Consumer cooperatives are regulated by its members. This chapter addresses the question: in terms of organizational effectiveness, are consumer cooperatives for members better off than cooperatives for the general public? It aims to explore and investigate collaborative SCM of consumer cooperatives. The research highlights the significance of the relationship between suppliers and consumers in the SCM of consumer cooperatives. The authors propose the hypothesis of the research as follows: In terms of the performance of the long-term contract between suppliers and customers, consumer cooperatives serving for members only are better than cooperatives serving for the general public. In order to verify and test the hypothesis, the methodologies employed are various from simulation modelling of 'system dynamics' to in-depth interviews and observations. The chapter concludes the competitive advantages of consumer cooperatives are serving for members only. This chapter will contribute theoretically and practically for consumer cooperatives. It also expands the scope of cooperative management studies from the perspectives of SCM.

In the final and concluding chapter (Seungkwon Jang, Ah Young Kim, Bo Young Oh, Jihyun Jeong), we are going to indicate what and how Korean consumer cooperative management matters in a wider context and for international readers. Considering relatively short periods of development, Korean consumer cooperatives are growing rapidly in the size and impact. Since the inception, consumer cooperatives have driven the shifting directions of not only Korean cooperatives in general but also Korean agricultural and retail industries. In sum, Korean consumer cooperatives have been playing a crucial role in social innovation of Korean society. The perspectives and conceptual models of Korean consumer cooperatives are the core value of this book.

The main body of the book, Chapters 2 through 7, can be summarized in Table 1.3, which indicates each chapters' key themes according to the Blueprint's five themes, as well as theories, methods, and findings.

Table 1.3 Summary of the chapters

Ch.	Title	Blueprint Theme	Key words	Theory	Method	Findings
2	Cooperative Governance Practice	Participation/ identity	Organization, governance	Sensemaking (Weick)	Case study	What is important in cooperative governance is not only the nominal and mechanical participation, but also the actual and practical decision-making competency that the cooperative governance.
3	Gender Perspectives for Consumer Cooperatives	Participation/ identity	Organization, gender	Gender theories (Calás and Smircich)	Literature review	More attention should be paid to such issues as the patriarchal organization culture and hierarchical relationships based on differences, not just to gender diversity.
4	Price Stability and Asymmetric Price Transmission for Agricultural Products	Identity/ sustainability	Finance	Asymmetric Price Transmission (Meyer and von Cramon-Taubadel)	Quantitative (Error correction model)	The asymmetry of price transmission in conventional agricultural products market is considerably alleviated under the pricing policy used by consumer cooperatives. Consumer cooperatives could contribute to enhance the welfare of producers as well as consumers by their stable pricing policy favourable to both producers and consumers.
5	Financing Consumer Cooperatives	Capital/ sustainability	Finance	The pecking order theory (Myers)	Case study	Consumer cooperatives have their own pecking order in financing, retained earnings, member loans, optional investment shares, and banks and external loans.
6	Consumer Cooperative Brand Identity	Identity/ participation	Marketing	Brand management model (de Chernatony)	Narrative analysis	There are common characteristics of the four consumer cooperatives' brand identities such as 'supply of safe and reliable food', 'fulfilment of the principles and values of cooperatives', and 'realization of human-centred alternative economy.
7	Member Participation and Productivity Changes	Participation/ sustainability	Operations	Theories of the firm	Quantitative (Malmquist output-based productivity index)	It is member participation in management and activities that has affected the productivity change. It is important to make members informed about shared values and shared goals of the cooperative, and provide a means for them to engage in activities through pertinent policies.
8	Consumer Cooperatives and Supply Chain Management	Sustainability/ participation	Supply chain management	Supply chain management (Mentzer et al.)	System dynamics	There is no need of benevolent behaviour of any particular supply chain entity when the organization can build trust in the whole supply chain through a good management structure.

Notes

1 http://eng.hansalim.or.kr/ (accessed 27th September 2018).
2 http://www.happycoop.or.kr/ (accessed 27th September 2018).
3 http://dure-coop.or.kr/ (accessed 27th September 2018).
4 http://www.icoop.or.kr/ (accessed 27th September 2018).
5 Happycoop has changed its name three times: *Hamkyeganeun Saenghyup* [Together cooperatives] *(1989), Yeosung Minwoohoe Saenghyup* [Women link cooperatives] (2000), then *Hangbok Jungsim Saenghyup* [Happy coop cooperatives] (2013). However, in this context, Happycoop would be used to indicate the organization to avoid any confusion.
6 http://www.happycoop.or.kr/ (accessed 27th September 2018).
7 iCOOP has changed its name three times: *Gyeongin Saenghyup Yondae* [The association of consumer cooperatives in Seoul and Incheon regions] (1997), 21st Century Consumer Cooperatives (1998), then iCOOP (2000).
8 'iCOOP' in official English name.
9 Chapter 2 is a revised and updated version of the article originally published in Korean: Kim, A. Y., Cho, Y.-J., and Jang, S. (2017) 'Hyeopdongjohabui geobeo-neonseu silcheon: Jeonju aikup sobijasaenghwalhyeopdongjohap saryeyeongu' [Cooperative Governance Practice: The Case of Jeonju iCOOP Consumer Cooperative]. *The Korean Journal of Cooperative Studies*, 34(3): 73–93.
10 Chapter 3 is a revised version of the presentation (Jang, S. and Kim, A. Y.) at the international research conference organized by the International Co-operative Alliance (ICA) Committee on Co-operative Research (CCR) in Pula, Croatia, on 25–28 June 2014.
11 Chapter 4 is a revised version of the presentation (Ji, M. and Choi, W) at the international research conference organized by the International Co-operative Alliance (ICA) Committee on Co-operative Research (CCR) in Pula, Croatia, on 25–28 June 2014.
12 Chapter 6 is a revised version of the presentation (Youn, S. and Lee, S.) at the international research conference organized by the International Co-operative Alliance (ICA) Committee on Co-operative Research (CCR) in Stirling, UK, on 20–24 June 2017.
13 Chapter 7 is a revised and updated version of the article originally published in Korean: Jung, S., and Choi, W. (2017) 'Johabwon chamyeowa sobijahyeopdong-johap saengsanseong byeonhwa: hansallimseoul sobijasaenghwalhyeopdongjo-habeul jungsimeuro' [Participation of Members and Changes in Productivity of Consumer Cooperatives: The Case of Hansalim Korea]. *Journal of the Korean Production and Operations Management Society*, 28(4): 391–415.
14 Chapter 8 is a revised version of the presentation (Kim, D., Park, S. and Jang, S) at *The International Conference of Cooperative Responses to Global Challenges* organized by Humboldt-Universität zu Berlin, in Berlin, Germany, on 21–23 March, 2012.

References

Dure Consumer Cooperatives' Union (2017, December) *Seumoosal Cheongnyun Dure Ttwieoneomgi* [Jumping Over 20-Year-Old Dure]. Seoul, Korea: Dure.
Hansalim (2018) *2018 Hansalim Story: Together Again And Fresher*. Seoul, Korea: Hansalim.
Hansalim Federation (2015, May) *Saengmyeongeul gakkuneun saramdeul Bangbang-gokgok Hansalim Saengsangongdongchae* [People Who Raise Life: Hansalim Producing Community Over Every Nook and Cranny of the Land]. Seoul, Korea: Hansalim.
Huh, M. Y. (2008) 'Saenghyeobui daeanjeog sobimunhwaui seonggyeoggwa geu hamui' [Alternative Consumption Culture and Implication of Consumer Coopera-tives]. *Nongchon sahoe* [Agricultural Society], 18(2): 7–36.

14 *Seungkwon Jang*

International Co-operative Alliance (2013) *Blueprint for a Co-operative Decade.*
    International Co-operative Alliance. https://ica.coop/sites/default/files/media_
    items/ICA%20Blueprint%20-%20Final%20version%20issued%207%20Feb%2013.
    pdf (accessed 30 August 2018).
Jang, S., Kim, A. Y., Son, B. K., and Kim, D. (2011) *A Secondary Co-operative for
    Organic Certification Service: A Case Study of the AFT in Korea.* ICA Global
    Research Conference, Mikkeli, Finland, 24–27 August.
Jang, S., Park, C., and Lee, S. H. (2004) *Chinhwangyeongnongsanmul yutongsiseutem
    gaeseoneul wihan yutong injeungje doip mit hwaryong* [Introduction and Imple-
    mentation of Distribution Certification System: Improving the Distribution System
    of Environmental-friendly Agricultural Products]. Unpublished Report, Seoul,
    Korea: Sungkonghoe University.
Jeong, E. M., Kim, D. H., and Kim, M. M. (2011, November) *Saenghyeob Gyeongje-
    saeobui Seonggwawa Jeongchaeggwaje* [Economic Fruits and Policy Tasks of Con-
    sumer Cooperatives in Korea]. Seoul, Korea: Hankook Nong-chon Gyeong-je
    Yeon-goo [Korea Rural Economic Institute].
Kim, H. M. (2017) 'The Experience of the Consumer Co-operative Movement in
    Korea: Its Break Off and Rebirth, 1919–2010.' In Hilson, M., Neunsinger, S.,
    and Patmore, G. (eds.), *A Global History of Consumer Co-operation Since 1850:
    Movements and Businesses.* Leiden, the Netherlands: Brill, pp. 353–378.
Kim, H. M., Yeom, C. H., Lee, M. Y., Jeong W. G., and Jeong, E. M. (2012)
    Hanguk Saenghwalhyeopdongjohap Undonge Giwongwa Jeongae [Consumer Co-
    operative: The Origin and Development of the Korea's Consumer Cooperative
    Movement]. iCOOP Co-operative Institute (ed.). Seoul, Korea: Purunnamu.
Kim, In-Sook (2012) 'Hang-bok Jung-sim Saenghyup, Saeroun Baldoteumae Bak-
    sooreul' [Happycoop, Applause for a New Start]. Ham-kye-ga-neun Yeo-sung
    [Women Going Together]. *Minwoohoe* [Women Link]. Seoul, Korea: Minwoohoe,
    no. 209. pp. 42–43.
Park, Young-sook (2007) 'Senghwalhyeobdongjohab: yeoseongui himeulo mandeun
    daeanjeog saengsangwa sobisiseutem' [Consumer Co-operative: Alternative Pro-
    duction and Consumption System by Women]. *Minwoohoe* [Women Link]. Seoul,
    Korea: Minwoohoe, pp. 179–206.
Yeom, Chan Hee (2018) 'iCOOP saenghyeobui Jeongchag Sigi' [The Settlement
    of iCOOP: From 1997 to 2007]. In iCOOP Co-operative Institute (eds.), *The
    Value and Practice of Cooperative People, Twenty Years Old iCOOP.* Seoul, Korea:
    iCOOP Co-operative Institute, pp. 11–79.

Websites

Dure Consumer Cooperatives' Union. (official website) http://dure-coop.or.kr/.
Hansalim. (official website) http://eng.hansalim.or.kr/.
Happycoop Co-operatives. (official website) http://www.happycoop.or.kr/.
Happycoop Co-operatives Story. (blog) http://happycoop.tistory.com.
iCOOP Consumer Co-operatives. (official website) http://icoop.coop/?page_id=
    7960499.
iCOOP UNION (2018) *20th iCOOP Net's Annual Report: iCOOP Creates Future
    Together.* Gunpo, Korea: iCOOP UNION [in English].
PTCoop. (official website). http://ptcoop.co.kr/.

2 Cooperative governance practice

Ah Young Kim, Young-Jeong Cho and Seungkwon Jang

I. Introduction

A cooperative is a member-owned and democratically governed enterprise, which shows different governance properties to those of corporations. Most cooperatives endeavor to realize democratic governance through a representative system, in which members of the organization elect delegates for monitoring business practices (Kim et al., 2013; Park, 2010; Seo, 2006; Spear, 2004; Cornforth, 2004). Cooperative governance is subject to diverse factors, such as the formal and informal structures of the Board of Directors (BODs), the decision-making process and so on (Choi et al., 2013), which indicates the significance of how the governance is actually practiced. In contrast to other types of organizations, BODs of cooperatives are normally composed of delegates of members ultimately responsible for representing interests of the members. BODs, therefore, mediate varied interests of multi-stakeholders and draw up the overall policies so as to efficiently retain businesses reflecting members' needs. This distinctive characteristic of BODs in cooperatives explains why the decision-making process of BODs, through which functions and beliefs of the directors are demonstrated should be studied as well as its structure.

Cooperative governance practice refers to the process in which multi-stakeholders build a consensus to achieve dual-purposes of cooperatives that are social and economic values. The consensus here means communication-based voluntary participation between members. Weick's sensemaking theory as a dynamic process of organization is applicable to understanding cooperative governance practice. Weick (1995) considers organization as a mechanism of making sense of changing situations and environments by which it is surrounded, not as static and prescriptive. Members of an organization resolve equivocality they face by creating shared meanings after repeating the process of creating and discarding different meanings. For sensemaking to be conducted successfully, there needs to be an interpretive framework shared through communication between organization members. Additionally, it is essential that those involved in the sensemaking process are aware of circumstances they confront in dialogues and narratives, as well as their own roles (Heifetz et al., 2009; Weick, 1995). To be able to provide a stable interpretive framework – that is, the sensemaking process – can be seen as a pivotal function that an organization ought to possess in order to survive. Cooperatives have a dynamic system that is affected by manifold situations, such as the history or culture of the society in which they exist. Thus, it is crucial to explore the process in which members of cooperatives create shared meanings as to ambiguity and uncertainty they frequently experience. The present research investigates cooperative governance practice and how board members in cooperatives internalize the cooperative values and principles. Particularly, a case of Jeonju iCOOP is analysed, where the BODs has turned a crisis into a promising opportunity.

II. Cooperative governance and sensemaking

1. *Cooperative governance and board of directors*

Cooperative governance has been relatively less theorized compared to corporate governance, which is generating many studies applying various competing theories of governance in the profit sector (Cornforth, 2004; Shaw, 2006). Corporate governance is the framework of rules, relationships, systems and processes within and by which authority is exercised and controlled in corporations. It encompasses the mechanisms by which companies, and those in control, are held accountable. In terms of corporate governance research, the BODs' role can vary each nation and also corporate within a nation; thus, there have been several attempts to analyze corporate governance through incorporating different perspectives (Jang, 2002).

According to Novkovic and Miner (2015), cooperative governance has three properties: humanism, joint ownership, control and democracy. Humanism is premised on stewardship theory that assumes executives to instinctively carry out the right things, rather than pursuing financial rewards or rational economic activities, which is different from agency theory that sees the agents and the principals in a conflict of interests. Cornforth (2002) suggests a synthesized perspective for research on cooperative governance and BODs. He has attempted to reinterpret governance of cooperatives and non-profit organizations with varied governance theories and argues that multiple perspectives encompassing heterogeneous theories are needed for BODs to perform both a role of enhancing the organization's performance and one of exercising the delegated authority with responsibility and deliberation. Another point is made by Miller and Abraham (2006) that there are diverse studies on corporate governance, while governance of third sector organizations is seldom dealt with. Due to the complexity of governance practice, furthermore, they point out that, because theoretically good governance and governance practice are different matters, a comprehensive governance theory should be established reflecting attributes of the third sector. Spear (2004) emphasizes the necessity of a new theory on member-owned and democratically governed organizations. Within member-owned organization such as cooperatives or mutuals, decision making is operated through representative democracy, in which the representativeness and legitimacy of the BODs could be diminished depending on whether the members participate in the process or not. To overcome the risk, he draws attention to the need of developing a new perspective that synthesize agency theory, which is a dominant theory in corporate governance research, and the participation of stakeholders, which is emphasized by member-owned organizations.

Cooperatives seek to achieve economic and social values for members' benefits so their governance shows dynamics. Especially, the board members as the delegates of the members of the organization are required to play a role of 'reflective practitioner'. Schön defines the reflective practitioner as one who can think while acting and thus can respond to the uncertainty, uniqueness and conflict involved in the situations in which professional practice (Schön, 1983). The boards of cooperatives set the organization's agenda and priorities through reviewing, approving and monitoring the organization's strategic direction as the ultimate keepers of the cooperative values and principles. They ought to define attributes of the issues confronting them and find clues about them via discussion to fulfill the organization's goals. Chait et al. (2004) argue that board members are not ineffective because they are confused about their role, but because they are dissatisfied with their role. They demonstrate three modes of governance of non-profit organizations: fiduciary mode, strategic mode and generative mode. When three modes of governance operate harmoniously, effective governance would be available. The three modes of governance give a useful source to establish a new perspective on cooperative governance. Type I, the fiduciary mode, is where BODs are concerned primarily with the stewardship of tangible assets. Type I constitutes the bedrock of governance – the fiduciary work intended to ensure that non-profit organizations are faithful to mission, accountable for performance, and compliant with relevant laws and regulations. Type II, the strategic mode, is where BODs develop a strategy with management to set the organization's priorities and course, and to deploy resources accordingly. Type III, the generative mode, is where BODs, along with executives, frame problems and make sense of ambiguous situations – which in turn shapes the organization's strategies, plans, and decisions. Because most organizations lack frameworks and practices for this work, it's easy for BODs to become bystanders to it – even though it is central to governance.

The nature of the three modes of governance is shown in Table 2.1. In fact, the generative mode suggests a more comprehensive perspective than fiduciary and strategic modes. An organization is not merely a rational strategy and logical planning but composed of cultural and political systems and symbolic context. Therefore, the BODs are expected to form a frame of given issues and chances within the organization, not to find an absolute solution, and understand the past and the present experiences of the organization by learning and retrospective thinking. Generative governance is called 'generative' because it is the *genesis* of the organization's work later translated into strategies, policies, plans, and tactics. Generative thinking provides a sense of problems and opportunities above and beyond what is normally experienced. This new understanding is achieved by questioning the frame through which problems and opportunities are seen.

Table 2.1 Three modes of governance

	Fiduciary mode	*Strategic mode*	*Generative mode*
Organization type	Bureaucratic	Open system	Non-rational
Leadership	Hierarchical	Analytical	Reflective
Main purpose of BODs	Stewardship of tangible assets	Strategic partnership with management	Source of leadership for organization
Main tasks of BODs	Technical: oversee operations, ensure accountability	Analytical: shape strategy, review performance	Creative: discern problems, engage in sensemaking
Role of BODs	Sentinel	Strategist	Sense-maker
Performance measurement	Facts, figures, finances reports	Strategic indicators, competitive analysis	Sign of learning and discerning

Source: Chait et al. (2004) revised.

Cooperatives aim for democratic governance based on voluntary participation, whereas members are motivated to participate by both internal and external factors and subject to external environments. Particularly, the purposes of cooperatives are multi-layered, complex, abstract and fluid. A goal considered highly important at a time could become less important at another time and a task that a member thinks of as the top priority might be of little importance to another member. In other words, goals are not an unchangeable constant that regulates other variables but needs to be continuously reviewed and modified through a mutual understanding and action of stakeholders.

Kanter (1984) argues that reframing the past leads to the ability to establish the future. Mintzberg et al. (2005) insist that the strategy occurs during the process of ongoing businesses, not from the formal planning process which frames detailed directions of the organization by presupposing the present to the future situations. People think retrospectively and acknowledge new patterns in dominant routines that have already existed but not by forming the frame of interpretation, from which new meanings are derived. Consequently, it can be said that cooperative governance, aiming to lead the organization to its goals and direction arranged by the board, is generative governance, which identifies given issues and provides different frames of interpretation to generate an alternative way of thinking. Cooperative boards thus ought to construct the frame of the present problems and understand experiences in the past.

2.   *Sensemaking and communication*

Facing the streams of ambiguous events, people are encouraged to comprehend and make sense of what is happening (Heifetz et al., 2009). In such situations, ambiguity and uncertainty of the information they obtain initiate a sensemaking process to eliminate those attributes. Individuals' actions are premised on sensemaking and thereby the sensemaking process is crucial especially in dynamic and fluctuating environments (Maitlis, 2005). In that sense, sensemaking is regarded as one of the principal concepts in organizations that are more subject to changes in environments than individuals are.

According to Weick (1993), it is difficult that an individual living in an interdependent world determines one's behaviors by oneself entirely. Thus, a group of individuals creates a collective structure in interlocking form, which is referred to as an organization. Human beings are organized themselves in order to remove the uncertainty of knowledge they possess and the organization is created and maintained through communication and sensemaking (Salancik and Pfeffer, 1978; Kreps, 1986; Weick, 1995). Sensemaking, as stated by Feldman and March (1981), refers to the process of sharing meanings for members to understand the organization: what is the organization; what is the organization good at and unskilled at; what kinds of problems do we face and how can we solve them. Therefore, sensemaking is social process aiming at making interpretation and giving an explanation of cues in the streams of events, rather than exerting the influence on the evaluation of choice (Laroche, 1995; Lant, 2002; Weick, 1993; Weick, 2005). A story generated from sensemaking is considered relative as ways of interpreting experiences to vary according to changing contexts and members engaging in the process. Thus, members of the organization are meant to learn and create a plausible story from those concerning in the organizing process, not to find a particular one that already exists (Gioia and Thomas, 1996).

Weick (1993) argues that a particular process is necessary to derive collectively structured common actions from shared meanings between members of the organization. First of all, the organization is formed by the interplay between those who pursue different goals, not those having the same goal. When initiating the formation of an organization, there needs to be a collectively structured action, that is, interdependency as a common means; what is essential for the members with diverse goals is exploitation of the shared process, not the pursuit of the common goal. Subsequently, members of the organization begin to converge upon the interlocking action, which leads to the conversion from various goals to a shared one. The shared goal plays a role as a means by which the individuals achieve what they want and its successful operation as the means depends on intersubjectivity that enables effective communication between the members. The organization has undergone the processes explained above finally retains the capacity to carry out various means and each member of the organization adopts a unique way that is adequate for their own proficiency to fulfill the common goal through the division of labor between the members. Such a circular process occurs repeatedly in the process of the organization's goal being diversified.

The members inevitably encounter several negotiations between them over a long period of time to build a consensus of opinions on events. This activity can be referred to as 'consensual validation', through which the duality of the events diminishes (Weick, 1993). To understand the behavior of members within the organization, it is important to recognize thoroughly internal factors and a mechanism affecting the behaviors. Internal factors are a range of cognition of situations by which agents are surrounded, as well as one's own role, which takes place in the process of sensemaking (Weick, 1995). Sensemaking is related to how individuals simultaneously shape and react to the environment they face. In other words, sensemaking is a process in which individuals internalize and structure external stimuli into their own way of thinking, in order to interpret, understand, explain, infer and predict them. Also, it takes place when there is a set of stimuli from the environment. People try to understand what is going on when facing the streams of ambiguous events. And each makes decisions of what to do with their own set of answers. Thus, it is a key task to maintain the relationship between members and establish a common way of making sense that causes collective behavior.

The sensemaking process can be explained into three stages: enactment, selection, and retention. Once recognizing any noticeable difference from their environment, people begin to make sense of the change. The environmental change stimulates them to cognize their environment in different ways. The organization's members respond to physical context so as to objectively interpret it and through the response, or cognition, actively create the world they live. In such a process, they interact with and enact the context by the information they have and created meanings (Kreps, 1986). The members selectively recognise the context and become aware of the fact that their behaviours and the framework cognized in the past can influence their environment directly. Subsequently, a diverse range of interpretation of and response to the recognised context, generated by the members, gradually converges upon a common interpretation or response through selection. Among various possibilities, some are selected as being more useful and plausible than the others, thereby become routinized and sustained within the organization. It is noteworthy that each stage takes place not in sequential order but simultaneously and that elements that appear at each stage vary according to situations or contexts of the organization.

Weick et al. (2005) elaborate the conception of sensemaking by presenting its attributes. Firstly, sensemaking is initiated with situations with ambiguity and turbulence where there seems to be a possibility of change or trouble, but it is not straightforward to define it clearly. Secondly, active agents perceive cues of the problem and categorize them in their own distinctive way. Thirdly, they conceptualize and label the categorized to establish a common system for effective communication. Each agent individually categorizes and labels the cues and the process of selecting and discarding them is repeated. Fourthly, the extracted cues are reviewed in retrospect. By regarding preceding events as mistakes or opportunities, the problem can be interpreted in relation to the events in the past. To put it another way, understanding the past would lead to understanding the present and the future. Fifthly, agents make sense of the cues obtained from the situations. To make sense of something is a process of connecting abstract elements and concrete ones; interpretation and experiment that are abstract and personal are interlocked with concrete elements that are irrelevant to the attributes of the person who interprets and conducts the experiment on the cues (Paget, 1988). Lastly, as sensemaking is a social and systematic process, interdependency is embedded in it. Sensemaking is influenced by varied social factors including discourse with previously relevant people. And these social factors in return have an impact on the organization as a whole, which make the interdependent distribution of information possible.

Another attribute of sensemaking is systematization through communication. Communication is a key element of sensemaking; sensemaking is expanded and resources of language are produced via communication and discourses (Taylor and Van Every, 2000). In some respects, it can be said that sensemaking is fundamentally about communication (Jablin, 1982). Communication develops shared meanings and dissipates differences between interpretations generated by members of the organization before any structured behavior is collectively conducted (Donnellon et al., 1986). Weick (1993) shows that, through a case study on Mann Gulch fire incident, the absence of communication between members causes the deteriorated ability of the group to deal with the crisis, which results in failing to set up a team, and it was consequently followed by the fatal accident. Communication in part has a significant influence on a mechanism in which a consensus of meanings among the organization's members is created, retained and transferred.

3. Research propositions

The purpose of this research is to suggest a new perspective on explaining processes of cooperative's governance practice based on literature review. Generally, a case study is a research method preferred when the research question contains 'how' or 'why' (Yin, 2011). It is suitable to use this method when complex and detailed understanding is required while exploring the research issue or when to comprehend real-world problems (Cresswell, 2010). Therefore, this research sets two propositions based on the theoretical review and aims to expand the scope of cooperative governance research.

> Proposition 1: Cooperative governance is generative governance.
> Proposition 2: Generative governance is sensemaking based on communication.

III. The case of Jeonju iCOOP governance

This research is a qualitative case study in terms of concentrating on the governance practice of Jeonju iCOOP's board. Jeonju iCOOP is a consumer cooperative that is located in Jeonju, North Jeolla Province, in Korea. Qualitative research rests on a philosophical presupposition that a society is composed of individuals who interact with each other and involves observation of and interaction with those being studied, on their own domain and in their own language (Kirk and Miller, 2007). A prime focus placed by the qualitative study is a specific circumstance or person, and the language being used, rather than statistics, is emphasized (Maxwell, 2009). In particular, the case study method is preferred when discussing in-depth case and developing analyses through which provide thorough understandings of the circumstance and implicit meanings in it (Cresswell, 2010; Merriam, 2005).

This research tool is useful when distinctions between the observed phenomena and contexts are equivocal and when investigating the contemporary phenomena within the real-life context (Yin, 2011). Also, it aims to make a generalization of not the population being examined but the theories applied.

1. Jeonju iCOOP

Jeonju iCOOP is a primary consumer cooperative established in 2002, member of iCOOP, which is one of the most popular consumer cooperatives federations in Korea. As of 2018, 5,150 households, which account for 1.9% of the whole households in Jeonju, are members of the cooperative. It operates two stores selling environmental-friendly food and household items and runs an economic business of home delivery. The annual revenue in 2015 was about 4.6 billion KRW (1 USD = 1176.31 KRW as of 2015) and 35 workers were employed. Furthermore, Jeonju iCOOP implements diverse activities in which members can participate and those of public interest in social issues such as campaigns for honest food labeling and for healthy school lunches.

This chapter has explored a crisis Jeonju iCOOP confronted, which has been changed into a new opportunity afterward. Jeonju iCOOP might have lost the deposit and the working space but has solved these problems by moving their office to another region and transforming their office into a 'space for members'. Focusing on the affair of moving the office, this case study analyzing the governance practice of Jeonju iCOOP has been conducted in several ways. Firstly, it has scrutinized relevant materials like the proceedings of the board, the sourcebooks of the general meetings in 2015 and 2016, and so on. Secondly, the pre-questionnaires were distributed among 5 out of 10 board members who were able to participate in the survey, and interviews were proceeded with those who had answered the questionnaires. Two researchers engaged in the interviews as interviewers. One of the two researchers, who was serving consecutive terms for 4 years as the chief director, distributed the pre-questionnaires and the other conducted the face-to-face interviews with the 5 participants. The period of the interviews was from 10th to 14th of October 2016. The characteristics of the participants are shown in Table 2.2. And, finally, the documents, materials and the results of the interviews were analyzed individually and then synthesized.

Table 2.2 The interviewees

interviewee	Periods of being in office as a member of the board	Periods of participating in the cooperative movement
A	2 years (newly appointed)	3 years
B	2 years (newly appointed)	4 years
C	2 years (newly appointed)	4 years
D	3 years (consecutive)	5 years
E	3 years (consecutive)	6 years

2. *Jeonju iCOOP governance practice*

The BODs of Jeonju iCOOP cognizes the situation where they might lose their office and the deposit for it as a crisis and tried to find a solution through active interaction. Each board member was initially a member of the cooperative who joined Jeonju iCOOP to fulfill their own needs. By participating in activities of the cooperative such as the town meetings or the committees, they have built up experiences about and knowledge of the activities, based on which they were elected as the representative of members of the cooperative at the general meeting. The board directly gets involved in the overall management – namely, practical affairs, planning and proceeding activities, and so on.

The property-related task was not as frequent as other tasks. Thus, there were neither special training programs to improve the worker's expertise nor professional's advices. The contract term of the office was 5 years and renewed in 2015. Since the plan of moving the office to another place was being considered while renewing the contract, the renewed contract period was 1 year and the leaseholder and Jeonju iCOOP agreed upon renewal of the contract every year depending on their situations. In 2010 when making the contract, Jeonju iCOOP has not secured the leasehold rights, which were needed for the security deposit to be protected. And its reasons are unclear according to an interview. The person who was then in charge of the contract by accident had omitted that task and the BODs also did not recognize it. Furthermore, the issue as to the leasehold rights was not identified when renewing the contract.

The board members, who confronted the crisis that they might lose the deposit and space for their office, showed a positive interaction between each other during the process of solving the problem in order to overcome the absence of professional knowledge and the concern over the financial loss of members of the organization. Before the crisis, there were two regular meetings of the BODs every month, which, since the crisis, changed to not only the regular meetings of the BODs but also additional temporary meetings twice every month and sharing the situations and opinions through online messengers. Moreover, the roles for solving the problem were divided into teams and meetings by each team took place. When more than half of the members agree, the decision should be put into practice straightaway. The prompt answer of the board members to the problem as described previously is based on their responsibility as the representatives of members for preserving the organization's assets. According to the interviews, all of the board members emphasized that the office deposit was also one of the organization's assets and had the same stance on the issue that losing the deposit means the loss of the organization's members and so they had to resolve this problem well. Although the office related to this trouble was contracted in 2010, the board members who were then neither the board nor the organization's members considered it as one for which they are responsible. Such a strong sense of responsibility has consequently led to a positive result that they received the deposit back by persuading and negotiating with the leaseholder, despite the situation where it was legally impossible to secure the deposit. Also, these procedures have resulted in higher interest in property contract and thorough monitoring by the BODs and members on overall practical affairs of the organizational management as well as the related tasks.

In terms of making decisions on practical tasks including the location, the internal structure of the new office, the board members were still in charge. In this process, they looked for a place for the new office by voluntarily organizing a team and proceeded the discussion between the members. The board members throughout the problem-solving process internalized the cooperative values, considering that they represent the organization's members. Board member A said that she has come to think about one's role as the board member representing members of the organization by looking at other board members actively engaging in the process. Likewise, member B appreciated the efforts of other board members and resolved on making more contributions next time. While looking for a new office to move in, the BODs of Jeonju iCOOP realized a new meaning of the office as to the role of and what is most important about the office. While the office had originally been considered as a place for providing the basic office work and service, it was recognized in another sense that the office should play its role as a place for interactions between members of the organization.

Rather than raising questions to the faced difficulty such as 'what is wrong?' or 'what is the plan?', the BODs of Jeonju iCOOP asked themselves 'what is the problem?' and discussed actively what the office of cooperative should look like while dealing with the issue in moving the office. As a result, they connected the concept of cooperatives – a cooperative is an association by those who voluntarily gather together to resolve the common problems – with the concrete reality, not working out the problem in property by merely moving the office into a new place. The office constructed for providing the organization's members with administrative service has changed into space for members' meeting that induces cooperative within everyday living.

3.   *Sensemaking process of the BODs of Jeonju iCOOP*

Sensemaking is triggered in multidimensional environments and unfamiliar and contradictory situations. Through sensemaking processes, the organization's members develop shared meanings that help to create behaviors of the future. In the case of Jeonju iCOOP, the board members formalized the issues derived from the ecological change based on their own experiences and cognition. In the process of resolving the enacted problem, subsequently, never did a certain member suggest a solution and others agree on it, but they gradually generated a congruence in their opinions and created the new meaning of the space for members' gathering. Figure 2.1 shows how these processes can be depicted using Weick's sensemaking process framework.

A sensemaking process begins with changes in ecological environments. When opening a Natural Dream store, directly managed by the cooperative, in Jeonju in 2012, Jeonju iCOOP moved its office to the neighborhood of the store. It was a decision for efficiency in the store management because, when a store

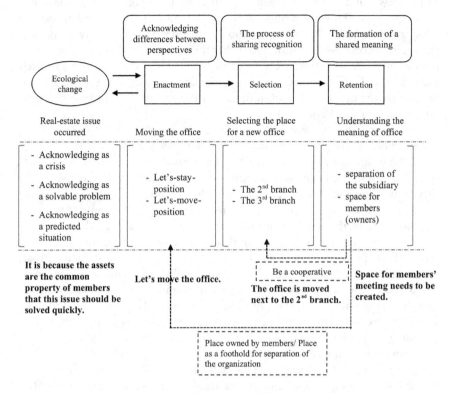

Figure 2.1 Sensemaking process of Jeonju iCOOP

opens, generally, the number of new members enrolling in the cooperative increases. Jeonju iCOOP that was running the store and the office in this area for four years had considered moving the office in terms of a critical mind that the office should be placed near a new store, but this issue was deferred as the establishment of a third store was delayed.

Around that time, the building in which the office resided was put up for auction, which made Jeonju iCOOP vulnerable to a significant loss of assets. And the board members became aware that cooperatives, which are non-profit organizations, are not relevant to law for the protection of commercial building tenants, and each member made a different interpretation of this situation. One considered the issue in the building put up for auction a critical crisis of the cooperative and put it as a priority to be solved, whereas another suggested that it could be resolved by, for instance, collecting money from the members in the worst scenario, and so was not an urgent problem. And another member regarded it as something to take in stride, as moving the office had been discussed before the problem emerged. As such, although each cognizance of the situation seemed various, they constantly shared the information about the situation and discussed it at an urgent board meeting from the point of the emergence of the problem. How they understand the situation varies depending on the actor, but the board members commonly agreed upon their duty to protect the organization's assets, which means that the representatives of members have responsibility for minimizing the financial loss. Although the extent to which each member had a sense of crisis about the circumstance that they might not be able to get the deposit back differed, all of the board members sought to find a solution for the loss.

In a chaotic environment within which ecological change has occurred, the organization's participants not only accept the physical situation objectively but also enact it through processes of creating information and meanings. The BODs of Jeonju iCOOP recognized the situation and its solution differently. Firstly, there was a position that if the landlord was unable to return the deposit back, it would be better to remain at the same place until it is guaranteed to get it back to avoid further costs occurring. In contrast, some argued that, before it is too late, moving the office into another area would be an optimal choice. In terms of solutions, there were various opinions suggested. Some opined that, when suffering the loss, the board members should contribute money to retain the assets, which are the common property of members, whereas others argued that the organization's members need to know about the problem and the loss should be recorded on the cooperative's account books. As such, even though they suggested solutions in various ways, the board members perceived through communication and reached a conclusion. The common opinion was 'to protect the organization's assets', for which the staff and the BODs constantly persuaded the landlord and eventually achieved the desired aim. Subsequently, the BODs of Jeonju iCOOP decided to move the office.

After enactment, there is a selection procedure where the enacted context cues are retrospectively selected and rationalized. The BODs, who had decided to move to another place, started to discuss where to move the office. It was for vitalizing activities such as societies and town meetings and motivating members to participate in them that the office was close to the store. The board members who had observed the positive influence of the closeness between the office and the store on members' participation proceeded, with a debate over to which store they would shift the office. As a result, the board members agreed upon moving into the second branch that had been previously considered.

The selected cues create and retain a shared meaning through a consensus identity within the organization. Such retention pursues not positivist rationality but consensus rationality commonly accepted by the actors. The formation of the shared meaning within the organization can routinize the organizational activities, and the actors' actions are stimulated by commonality and durability. How to understand the office has influenced the issue in where to transfer the office. If the office was considered merely as a place for administrative tasks and services for the organization's members, it would have been unnecessary to move it next to the store. That was not the case for the board members of Jeonju iCOOP, however. There were other perspectives, but they also showed a consensus about the role of the office as 'space for members' as well as for administrative tasks.

IV. Conclusion

This research has been initiated from an attempt to understand cooperative governance from a different point of view. The precedent studies have insisted a need of new perspectives for explaining cooperative governance practice, but there have been only a few studies that try to suggest either a theoretical or practical solution for this issue by dealing with cooperative governance practice. The present study based on the generative governance perspective has suggested the proposition that generative governance is sensemaking based on communication through the case of consumer cooperative governance practice and sought to explain it by the case study. To do so, the case of the BODs of Jeonju iCOOP, who has overcome the crisis, was analyzed exploratively, and the result of the analysis has shown that cooperatives establish generative governance in active communication, which is referred to as sensemaking.

In this study, Weick's sensemaking theory was applied in analyzing the process in which the cooperative board interacts with the ecological change and forms the generative governance, which consequently contributes to expanding the field of cooperative governance research. This study has produced a meaningful suggestion to research on governance in terms of perceiving organizations as dynamic systems, not as physical bodies or structures. What is important in cooperative governance is not only the nominal and mechanical participation but also the actual and practical decision-making competency that cooperative governance. Practically, it has its significance for focusing on cooperative governance practice. An issue in how to improve the capabilities of the representatives elected by the organization's members is placed at the core of practical tasks of cooperative governance. While a focal point of debates on the issue has been on ways to improve their proficiency in management, this study emphasizes particularly what proficiency should be required for the representatives of members. Such inquiry and exploration of answers to it are expected to have a positive impact on planning and developing educational programmes for the management of the BODs of cooperatives and the representatives of the organization's members.

References

Chait, R. P., Ryan, W. P., and Taylor, B. E. (2004) *Governance as Leadership: Reframing the Work of Nonprofit Boards.* Hoboken, NJ: John Wiley & Sons.

Choi, E. J., Choi, W., and Jang, S. (2013) 'Hyeobdongjohab isahoeui yeoghalgwa hyogwaseonge gwanhan gochal' [A Study on the Role of Board of Directors and Its Effectiveness in Cooperatives]. *The Korean Journal of Cooperative Studies*, 31(3): 73–92.

Cornforth, C. (2002) 'Making Sense of Co-operative Governance: Competing Models and Tensions.' *Review of International Co-operation*, 95(1): 51–57.

Cornforth, C. (2004) 'The Governance of Co-operatives and Mutual Associations: A Paradox Perspective.' *Annals of Public and Co-operative Economics*, 75(1): 11–32.

Cresswell, J. W. (2010) *Qualitative Inquiry and Research Design: Choosing Among Five Traditions.* Thousand Oaks, CA: Sage Publications, Inc.

Donnellon, A., Barbara G., and Michel G. B. (1986) 'Communication, Meaning and Organized Action.' *Administrative Science Quarterly*, 31(1): 43–55.

Feldman, M. S., and March, J. G. (1981) 'Information in Organizations as Signal and Symbol.' *Administrative Science Quarterly*, 26(2): 171–186.

Gioia, D. A., and Thomas, J. B. (1996) 'Identity, Image, and Issue Interpretation: Sensemaking During Strategic Change in Academia.' *Administrative Science Quarterly*, 41(3): 370–403.

Heifetz, R., Grashow, A., and Linsky, M. (2009) 'Leadership in a Crisis.' *Harvard Business Review*, 87(7/8): 62–69.

Jablin, F. M. (1982) 'Formal Structural Characteristics of Organizations and Superior Subordinate Communication.' *Human Communication Research*, 8(4): 338–347.

Jang, S. (2002) 'Jisiggieobui jibaegujo: hangug inteonesgieobui salyeyeonguleul jungsimeulo' [Corporate Governance of Internet Business Company in Korea]. *Korean Journal of Management*, 10(1): 161–193.

Kanter, R. M. (1984) *Change Masters.* New York: Simon and Schuster.

Kim, A. Y., Choi, E. J., and Choi, W. (2013) 'Hangug sobijasaenghwalhyeobdongjohab isahoeui teugseonge gwanhan siljeung yeongu' [An Empirical Study on Characteristics of Board of Directors in Consumer Co-operatives]. *The Korean Journal of Cooperative Studies*, 31(1): 27–55.

Kirk, J., and Miller, M. (2007) *Reliability and Validity in Qualitative Research.* Thousand Oaks, CA: Sage Publications, Inc.

Kreps, G. L. (1986) *Organizational Communication: Theory and Practice.* New York, NY: Longman Publishing Group.

Lant, T. K. (2002) 'Organizational Cognition and Interpretation.' In Baum, J. A. (ed.), *The Blackwell Companion to Organizations.* Oxford: Blackwell, pp. 344–362.

Laroche, H. (1995) 'From Decision to Action in Organizations: Decision-Making as a Social Representation.' *Organization Science*, 6(1): 62–75.

Maitlis, S. (2005) 'The Social Processes of Organizational Sensemaking.' *Academy of Management Journal*, 48(1): 21–49.

Maxwell, J. A. (2009) *Qualitative Research Design: An Interactive Approach.* Thousand Oaks, CA: Sage Publications, Inc.

Merriam, S. (2005) *Qualitative Research and Case Study Applications in Education.* San Francisco, CA: Jossey-Bass Publishers.

Miller, M., and Abraham, A. (2006) *Towards the Development of Integrative Governance Framework for the Third Sector.* Paper presented at the 8th Biennnial Conference of Australia & New Zealand Third Sector Research, Adelaide.

Mintzberg, H., Ahlstrand, B., and Lampel, J. (2005) *Strategy Safari: A Guided Tour Through the Wilds of Strategic Management.* New York, NY: Simon and Schuster.

Novkovic, S., and Miner, K. (2015) *Co-operative Governance Fit to Build Resilience in the Face of Complexity.* Brussels: International Co-operative Alliance.

Paget, M. (1988) *The Unity of Mistakes: A Phenomenological Interpretation of Medical Work.* Philadelphia, PA: Temple University Press.

Park, J. K. (2010) 'Hyeobdongjohab isahoeui chaegimgwa yeoghal: migug nonghyeob salyeleul jungsimeulo' [The Responsibilities and Roles for Cooperative Boards of Directors: A Case Study of Agricultural Cooperatives in U.S.]. *The Korean Journal of Cooperative Studies*, 28(2): 28–47.

Salancik, G. R., and Pfeffer, J. (1978) 'A Social Information Processing Approach to Job Attitudes and Task Design.' *Administrative Science Quarterly*, 23(2): 224–253.

Schön, D. A. (1983) *The Reflective Practitioner: How Professionals Think in Action.* London: Temple Smith.

Seo, J. I. (2006) 'Hyeobdongjohab jibaegujoui gaeseon banghyang' [A Study on the Management Control System of Cooperatives in Korea]. *The Korean Journal of Cooperative Studies*, 23(2): 101–111.

Shaw, L. (2006) *Overview of Corporate Governance Issues for Co-operatives.* Paper presented at the Global Corporate Governance Forum, London, UK.

Spear, R. (2004) 'Governance in Democratic Member-Based Organizations.' *Annals of Public and Cooperative Economics*, 75(1): 33–60.

Taylor, J., and Van Every, J. (2000) *The Emergent Organization: Communication As Its Site and Surface.* Mahwah, NJ: Routledge.

Weick, K. E. (1993) 'The Collapse of Sensemaking in Organizations: The Mann Gulch Disaster.' *Administrative Science Quarterly*, 38(4): 628–652.

Weick, K. E. (1995) *Sensemaking in Organizations.* Third Edition. Thousand Oaks, CA: Sage Publications, Inc.

Weick, K. E., Sutcliffe, K. M., and Obstfeld, D. (2005) 'Organizing and the Process of Sensemaking.' *Organization Science*, 16(4): 409–421.

Yin, R. K. (2011) *Case Study Research: Design and Methods.* Third Edition. London and Singapore: Sage Publications, Inc.

3 Gender perspectives for consumer cooperatives

Ah Young Kim and Seungkwon Jang

I. Introduction

As the members of Korea's consumer cooperatives have been increasing recently, women are actively engaged in cooperative movement and enterprises at the same rate. The ratio of women members in Korea's consumer cooperatives is 89%, women directors about 77% in 2013 (Kim, 2013). And boards of directors of major consumer cooperatives indeed have significantly higher women's involvement than other organizations: iCOOP 100%, Hansalim 77.4%, Dure 69.2%, Happycoop 72.7% in 2018.[1] It is relatively higher than the ratio of other countries' women directors, such as the Asia Pacific region, which is just 23% in 2017 (ICA-AP, 2017).

However, the survey data alone are not enough to elaborate on the women-dominated consumer cooperative landscape of Korea. If gender ratio matters, consumer cooperatives could ironically try to increase the number of male members. Accepting conventional wisdom, however, the real gender issue in Korea is male-dominant organizational culture, regenerating patriarchal organizations. This paper provides a theoretical explanation of Korea's female-dominated cooperatives, as well as practical suggestions for a better cooperative enterprise.

There has been a growing number of researches on organization and management in relation to gender in Korea. The studies are largely based on the perspective of gender-as-variable. Gender is regarded as a demographic variable, which reflects significantly on managerial performances. These papers are highlighting men's dominance over women in number. The term 'gender' is gaining popularity. Its meaning was once used to refer to the social expectations and roles attributed to or experience by people based on their biological sex. But gender is taking on a much broader and more diffuse set of meanings. It has become a general label for talking about women, men, the relationship between them, related aspects of organizing, processes through which gender-differentiated behavior patterns are enacted and associated issues of power in various guises.

Sex and sex differences are still often naturalized as fixed or almost fixed in biology. The distinction between sex and gender was recognized in the 1960s in feminist and other critical accounts of women's and men's positions in society. These highlighted how what was often thought of as natural and biological was also social, cultural, historical and political. Oakley (1972) was among the first to distinguish 'sex' as biological sex differences from 'gender' as socio-cultural constructions of sex differences. The sex-gender approaches have prompted path-breaking work on gender relations, some attending to attitudes, self-concept and identity; others focusing on social categories and structural relations. In this, gender has often been understood as a way of recognizing socio-cultural relations and as relatively autonomous from biology. Such approaches articulate structural concepts of gender relations as in sex-gender classes, patriarchy, gender orders. Nonetheless, most of the gender research has an in-built assumption and part of the design, which is privileging the men/women distinction. And there is rather little chance of discovering if the people being studied divide up the social world in ways where the sex distinction is not crucial. There often appears to be little space in, for example, gender qualitative research for findings in which the distinction 'men' and 'women' is not crucial (Billing and Alvesson, 1994). A social constructivist understanding gender can be developed through the avoidance of the biological approach. We suggest a move away from 'body counting' as a basis for gender perspective organization and management studies.

This chapter discusses the alternative understandings of women-dominated consumer cooperatives. We present an overview of how the gender perspective of organization and management research has developed. And we examine characteristics of Korea's consumer cooperatives and gender in cooperatives research to explore and provide the necessity of gender perspective for future cooperative research.

II.   Gender and organizations

1.   *Different perspectives on gender*

Feminists in the 1970s strategically distinguished the difference between sex as a natural structure and gender as a social concept. More exactly, by asserting that while sex is inalterable since it is universal and natural, gender, a social and cultural construct, can be changed, they tried to spread the injustice of discrimination against women and improve the situation. Gender has been understood as the social order imposed differently on men and women, and utilized as a category to analyze society. On the other hand, doubt was cast upon the concept of gender. West and Zimmerman (1987) argued that gender is an emergent feature of social situations, not something one 'has' as an individual, but something humans 'do' in relation to each other as an ongoing accomplishment in social life. Sex is not meant as a relevant social category and is produced as a socially relevant by agreeing. In these theoretical approaches, gender differences are not a matter of perceptions when people face each other in organizations. Rather, organizations are already gendered as people enter them and people and organizations are part and parcel of a social system based on historical hierarchical differentiation by sex, class and race (Anderson, 1996). In the late 1980s, a view appeared that cast doubt on the sex/gender distinction, seeing both sex and gender as a form of knowledge and something constructed. Tavris (1992) indicated the problem of asking about men/women differences in the question of 'How are men and women different and who is superior?' and suggested that the question should be 'Who does it benefit to note and discuss the difference between men and women?' Won (2004) viewed gender not merely as a property of humans but also as a kind of social dynamic, based upon social relations. Furthermore, because the power relations in operation based on gender imply the inferiority of femininity to masculinity, not only men's experience but also women's and the relations between them need to be discussed in order to promote a balanced understanding of the organization.

Calás and Smircich (2006) viewed gender not as one of the demographic variables but as a conceptual frame of analysis, subject to change depending on the theory. They asserted that gender is closely related to feminist theories, which reveal unequal gender relations and seek to change them. Based on this, they summed up sex and gender conceptualized by each feminist theory and their meaning in organizations.

Firstly, liberal feminism, which emphasizes equal education and roles of men and women, consider gender as socially constructed sexuality and organizations as gender neutral, which are established to maintain the social order. On the other hand, in radical feminism, which advocates a new order where women are not subordinated to men, sex is viewed as the cause of women's oppression and gender as a social construction to maintain women's subordination. The organization maintains gender discrimination through patriarchal order. According to psycho-analytic feminism, sex is identified in the psychosexual stages of development of individuals and gender is constructed by the psychosexual stages of development influenced by the male-centered social structure. Organizations reproduce patriarchal stages of psychosexual development. Socialist feminism, which explains women's oppression by integrating capitalism and patriarchy, suggested that gender is socially constructed by the discrimination between sexes, races and classes, and ideology under patriarchal capitalism and organizations are power relations systems of genders, races and classes. Poststructuralist/postmodern feminism, which insists on deconstructing the male-centered, standardized notion of sex, regarded sex and gender as discursive practices constructed by the power, the resistance and the materiality of the human body, and suggested that objective conditions and circumstances of organizations construct gender and other discourses. Transnational/post-colonial feminism, which analyses and criticizes how Western-centric knowledge constructed the identities of the third-world women, suggested that the ways in which the third-world women could construct diverse subjects should be considered, overcoming the Western-centric knowledge of sex and gender and that organizations and transnational companies are the actors that perpetuate modern racial, gender relations.

2. Gender in organizational and management research

Marshall (1995) suggested that the increase of research that includes women as a variable was accompanied by an expansion in the number of subjects and areas of study such as studies on gender discrimination in organizations, male-dominated organizational cultures, or the male and masculinity. She also analyzed that studies from the doing-gender perspective were growing in number while, initially, there had been more studies setting gender as a fixed variable. Marshall indicated that gender-related research in the management and organization area, however, was still considered very unusual. Also, a lot of gender-related studies were putting their efforts proving the lack of differences between men and women, although it would be impossible to answer the questions of male-female differences without changing male domination and gender role stereotypes.

Broadbridge and Hearn (2008) have classified the trends of management and organization studies according to the gender perspectives for the last 30 years. Between the late 1970s and the early 1980s, there were studies on women in workplaces and the sexual division of labor, influenced by Marxist political economics and socialist feminism.

Kanter (1977) analyzed the status of women in the workplaces, and Ferguson (1984) examined the male-dominated bureaucracy and women. Kanter (1977), in a case study on American corporations, highlighted the difficulties that women face as token managers and showed how men pose gender role stereotypes on women by means of informal networks and so forth. Since the late 1980s, there have been attempts to differentiate sex from gender, influenced by the growth in the number of feminist studies on sexuality and identity, and based on that, research has been conducted on the sexual division of labor and organizational processes. Acker (1990, 2011) analyzed how organizations are gendered through symbols and images and the interactions among the members. Since the 1990s, influenced by the critical approach and plurality of feminism, studies have been conducted on gender discrimination in organizations and the resistance and challenge against it. In addition, studies focused on debates over gender discrimination in information and communication technology, gender and diversity, and diversity management. The authors argue that more studies were carried out in the areas of organizational behavior, organization theory, and human resources management than in marketing, finance, international management, and production management. In a review of studies on organization and management published in the *British Journal of Management* for 25 years, Broadbridge and Simpson (2011) suggested that study trends highlighting the lack of difference between men and women changed the direction in the mid-1990s towards a new approach to assessing the difference between them.

While previous studies emphasized the discrimination experienced by women in the organization, women's strength arising from the difference between men and women was highlighted by the following studies. Their major research subjects included women's voice, gendered organizational cultures, masculinity and the 're-masculinization', and gender as a process. The authors also propose three key priorities in terms of broad areas of research. Firstly, drawing on the methodologies and epistemologies inherent within women's voice literature, research must continually monitor gender difference in order to inform policy and practice and identify. The second is to 'tease out' and conceptualize emerging gendered hierarchies and how they take new forms. The third key focus for gender and management research is to reveal hidden aspects of gender and the processes of concealment within norms, practices, and values.

Calás and Smircich (2014) focused on the trajectory of gender and organization literature and how it has changed with the purpose of reclaiming the potential for social change that marked its beginning. They identified two main meta-theoretical approaches in gender and organization literature. The first approach – theorizing gender in organizations – follows a more 'naturalistic' or 'common-sense' orientation towards gender and understands sex as a biological characteristic and gender as social or cultural categorization usually associated with a person's sex. The second approach – gendering organization – 'denaturalizes' the common sense of gender using processual, social constructionist theoretical approaches. Mostly, gender in organization theorizing is framed through liberal humanist assumptions that abstract individualism sustains the possibility of a meritocratic society, and that gender neutrality and objective outcomes are assumed to be the norm. In contrast, gendering organization theory is framed through critical, mostly feminist philosophies, including socialist and poststructuralist theorization often addressing the historical and cultural reproduction of a patriarchal system where domination and inequality are the norms.

These two different approaches start from fundamentally different ontological and epistemological assumptions about sex and gender. Thus, organizational research on sex/gender would also be framed through substantially different methodologies (Calás and Smircich, 2009). Research from the gendering organizations perspective proceeds by scrutinizing how gender and difference are done, how organizations become gendered under these processes, and their power effects. In this case, it would be appropriate to apply methodologies and methods that are equivalent to those of ethnomethodology and institutional ethnography.

III.   Gender and Korea's consumer cooperatives

1.   *Characteristics of Korea's consumer cooperatives*

Since 1929, consumer cooperatives in Korea have formed their unique characteristics as follows. Firstly, they are closed cooperatives where only the members are entitled by the state law[2] to use the service. While consumer cooperatives in other countries do not restrict non-members from using their service, those in Korea and Japan have the policy that only their own members are eligible for the use of the service. Such feature has both positive and negative effects. Closed membership functions as an obstacle to their efforts to promote the public interest and generate profit; it also reinforces the bonds among members, helping with the democratic operation, autonomy and independence of the organization. Recently claims have been raised that it is problematic to legally restrict the eligibility to use the service in light of autonomy of the members and that the relevant laws should be revised so that the cooperatives can decide on the eligibility criteria.

Secondly, business items are generally limited to eco-friendly products and organic food. It is due to the social conditions in the 1970s when consumer cooperatives in Korea came back to life and to the demand of the consumer members, following a very distinctive pattern in comparison to consumer cooperatives in other countries, which freely sell the same items as the general markets.

Thirdly, consumer cooperatives in Korea are characterized by a strong notion of social movement. While other consumer cooperatives in the world started from the demand of low-wage workers with the main purpose of supplying products in good quality at affordable prices, those in Korea began their business to deal with social issues in relation to agriculture, the environment and food safety, when the social awareness on consumer cooperative movement was still very low.

Fourthly, women are actively involved in political activities. In Korea, women's participation in the labor force is in stagnation due to the economic recession. Women's participation in economic activities rose slightly from 49.3% to 52.3% during the eleven-year period from 2001 to 2012. Also, Korea's gender wage gap is the widest among the 35 OECD member nations. Especially, women's economic and social activities decrease suddenly after marriage due to the Korean family culture, where women assume full charge of housework and childcare. After their children become a certain age, Korean women's desire for economic and social activities increase. Thus, Korean women are willing to involve in cooperative movement and enterprises. Along with the socio-cultural shift, consumer cooperatives are providing them with opportunities for meaningful activities.

2. Gender in cooperative research

In this chapter, we analyzed relevant studies on women and gender among the 418 articles published in the *Korean Journal of Cooperative Studies* between 1983 and 2013. As a result of our analysis, we have discovered that there were little studies on women and gender in relation to consumer cooperatives. A total of 2.9% of the studies were on consumer cooperatives, and only one of them discussed a woman-dominated board of directors in consumer cooperatives. Empirically analyzing the relationship between governance and performance, Kim et al. (2013) observed the female-dominated BODs in Korean consumer cooperatives and suggested that this characteristic should be studied further in relation to the economic and social activities of Korean women. Other studies on consumer cooperatives mainly attempted to approach the implication of relevant laws, the business of consumer cooperatives and their aspects of the social movement. The tendency of lack of interest in women and gender is also found in the research area of organizations and management, which may indicate how the patriarchal culture of Korea has influenced the knowledge production process.

Reflecting the realistic limitation of the lack of interest in women and gender, studies on cooperatives related to women and gender were also examined. In studies on other types of cooperatives, only a few of them were discussing women and gender; there have been only three articles related to women and gender published in *The Korean Journal of Cooperative Studies* for the last 30 years. All of them were on female education programs conducted by the farmers' cooperative and credit unions, attempting empirical analysis with male and female as variables similar to the education level and age. They all used the approach of gender in organizations, conceptualizing the experience of the women in the programs into figures or general terms. Given that gender is not a fixed variable but a social construction, however, a different approach is needed, for instance, in order to reveal gendering taking place within organizations and its reproduction.

IV. Conclusion

Along with the increased economic and social activities of women in Korea, there are a growing number of studies on organization and management in relation to gender and women. Most studies treat women and gender as the same concepts, using them as a demographic variable just as age or educational level. However, the concepts of sex and gender are distinct: while *sex* means biologically different men and women, *gender* means relations between male and female created by society and is a concept that encompasses social identities such as masculinity and femininity.

The concept of gender is changing in close relation to feminist theories and is gradually expanding its meaning. In light of this trend, studies on gender and organizations can be classified into two categories: 'theorizing gender in organizations approach' and 'gendering organization approach.' The former regards sex and gender as stable human properties, compares the structured circumstances influencing men and women in different ways, and seeks to rectify the inequality. The latter focuses on the creation and reproduction of the hierarchical order that acknowledges the superiority of a specific sex determined on the basis of biological criteria. In particular, noting how taken-for-granted social categories are naturalized with gendering effect, this approach explores the dichotomous division based on differences and the creation of hierarchical order, and the knowledge production process involved.

The membership of consumer cooperatives in Korea mainly consists of women with high demand for eco-friendly produce and safe food. They are highly interested in social values such as eco-friendly food and preservation of the agricultural production infrastructure. As most of them are housewives who participate in the activities and management of the cooperatives, the rate of female members on the board of directors is high. In Korean society, as a patriarchal culture, the case of consumer cooperatives is considered unique in that women's economic and social participation is so active. This study thus attempted to interpret those characteristics of consumer cooperatives from the perspective of gender, analyzing studies on consumer cooperatives in relation to women and gender. This led us to observe the lack of attention to women and gender in studies on consumer cooperatives in Korea, with most studies concentrating on the approach of theorizing gender in organizations.

For alternative understandings of women-dominated consumer cooperatives in Korea, the authors suggested gender perspectives. Gender is not a property of humans but a social dynamic, and is based upon social relations. Therefore, because discriminative perceptions and dichotomous divisions based upon them are in operation in the background of gender relations, not only men's experience but also women's and the relations between them need to be discussed in order to promote a balanced understanding of organizations and cooperatives. Thus, beyond the dichotomous division of men and women, more studies are needed from gender perspectives, which analyze the process and context within the division and pay attention to the knowledge production process as well.

Especially, if the Korean consumer cooperatives' characteristic of female domination was approached in the light of excessively female-oriented participation, it would lead to a solution of balancing the gender ratio through more male participation. Such a solution, however, has the limitation of not being able to approach the practical gender issues of the male-centric organization culture and the reproduction of patriarchal organizations. Therefore, in order to better understand consumer cooperatives in Korea, more attention should be paid to such issues as the patriarchal organization culture and hierarchical relationships based on differences, not just to gender diversity. Therefore, it is necessary to denaturalize and understand how the formal structures have been hierarchically organized along gender lines. Also, further critical research is needed, which deals with a wide range of organizational actors, regardless of whether they are in positions of authority.

Notes

1 Korea's major consumer cooperative federations' websites in 2018.
  http://www.icoop.coop/.
  http://www.hansalim.or.kr/.
  http://www.dure-coop.or.kr/.
  http://www.happycoop.or.kr/.
2 The Korean government enacted the Consumer Cooperative Act in 1998 and amended it in 2010.

References

Acker, J. (1990) 'Hierarchies, Jobs, Bodies: A Theory of Gendered Organizations.' *Gender & Society*, 4(2): 139–158.

Acker, J. (2011) 'Gendering Organizational Theory.' In Steven, J., Shafritz. J., and Jang, Y. S. (eds.), *Classic Readings in Organization Theory*, Boston, MA: Wadsworth, pp. 480–488.

Anderson, C. D. (1996) 'Understanding the Inequality Problematic: From Scholarly Rhetoric to Theoretical Reconstruction.' *Gender & Society*, 10(6): 729–746.

Billing, Y. D., and Alvesson, M. (1994) *Gender, Managers and Organizations*. Berlin and New York, NY: Walter de Gruyter.

Broadbridge, A., and Hearn, J. (2008) 'Gender and Management: New Directions in Research and Counting Patterns in Practice.' *British Journal of Management*, 19: 38–49.

Broadbridge, A., and Simpson, R. (2011) '25 Years On: Reflecting on the Past Looking to the Future in Gender and Management.' *British Journal of Management*, 22(3): 470–483.

Calás, M., and Smircich, L. (2006) 'From the Woman's Point of View Ten Years Later: Towards a Feminist Approach to Organization Studies.' In Clegg, S. R., Hardy, C., Lawrence, T. B., and Nord, W. L. (eds.), *The Sage Handbook of Organization Studies*. Second Edition. London: Sage, pp. 284–346.

Calás, M., and Smircich, L. (2009) 'Feminist Perspectives on Gender in Organizational Research: What Is and Is Yet to Be.' In Buchanan, D. and Bryman, A. (eds.), *Handbook of Organizational Research Methods*. London: Sage, pp. 246–269.

Calás, M., and Smircich, L. (2014) 'Theorizing Gender-and-Organization: Changing Times . . . Changing Theories?.' In Savita, K., Simpson, L., and Burke, R. J. (eds.), *The Oxford Handbook of Gender in Organizations*. London: Oxford University Press, pp. 17–52.

Ferguson, K. (1984) *The Feminist Case Against Bureaucracy*. Philadelphia, PA: Temple University Press.

ICA-AP (2017) *Gender Is More than a Statistic: Status of Women in the Cooperatives of the Asia Pacific Region*. Unpublished Report. New Delhi: The International Co-operative Alliance-Asia Pacific.

Kanter, R. M. (1977) *Men and Women of the Corporation*. New York, NY: Basic Books.

Kim, A. Y., Choi, E. J., and Choi, W. (2013) 'Hangung sobijasaenghwalhyeopdongjoham isahoeui teukseonge gwanhan siljeungyeongu' [An Empirical Study on Characteristics of Board of Directors in Consumer Cooperatives]. *The Korean Journal of Cooperative Studies*, 31(1): 27–55.

Kim, J. M. (2013) *Seoul yeoseonghyeopdongjoham saengtaegye yeongu* [A Study on the Social Ecosystem of Seoul Women's Cooperatives]. Seoul, Korea: Seoul Foundation of Women & Family.

Marshall, J. (1995) 'Gender and Management: A Critical Review of Research.' *British Journal of Management*, 6: 53–62.

Oakley, A. (1972) *Sex, Gender and Society*. London: Temple Smith.

Tavris, C. (1992) *Mismeasure of Woman*. New York, NY: Simon and Schuster.

West, G., and Zimmerman, D. H. (1987) 'Doing Gender.' *Gender & Society*, 1(2): 125–151.

Won, S. Y. (2004) 'Yeoseongjuuijeong jojigyeongu' [Feminist Organization Research Alternative]. *Korean Public Administration Review*, 38(6): 287–304.

4 Price stability and asymmetric price transmission for agricultural products

Minjin Ji and Woosuk Choi

I. Introduction

In a typical industry market, we commonly observe 'asymmetric price transmissions' (APT), in which output prices tend to respond rapidly or fully to input prices when they increase than when they decrease. This tendency is regarded as evidence of imperfect competition and is intensified in the market where the distribution process is long and complex. The asymmetric price transmission would cause a significant loss in the welfare of consumers, which are the endpoint in the distribution process when prices are highly volatile like agricultural product prices.

A cooperative is an autonomous association of persons united voluntarily to meet their common economic, social, and cultural needs and aspirations through a jointly owned and democratically controlled enterprise. Consumer cooperatives could play an important role even in sustaining the economic benefits of members from their businesses, and it could be interpreted in terms of the consumers' welfare.

Consumer cooperatives in Korea have been serving their members mainly with eco-friendly and organic agricultural products, and have been trying to provide those at a stable year-round price based on contract farming. That is because consumer cooperatives were developed from the direct transactions of organic agricultural products between consumers and producers as a part of a social movement in Korea (Jeong, 2006). iCOOP, one of the federations born in the movement, has been growing by leaps and bounds for the last fifteen years. They have focused on both organizing consumers as an association and improving the capacity of management as an enterprise (Choi et al., 2014).

As consumer cooperatives including iCOOP grow in revenue as well as membership, the issue of their social impact becomes significant, especially in terms of the consumers' welfare. While cooperatives as an enterprise should attain the economy of scale in order to keep sustainability, they have to try to keep their identity as an association for members. iCOOP has revised the pricing system of agricultural products to guarantee producers a reasonable income while providing consumers with their products at a stable price. It was designed to sustain the economic benefits for both of members and producers who are the counterpart in contract farming. Therefore, iCOOP presents a case to show the possibility of an effective pricing system for the economic benefits of the persons interested.

This chapter aims to investigate whether the pricing policy of consumer cooperatives mitigates the degree of asymmetric price transmission in agricultural products markets. Furthermore, we examine how consumer cooperatives could protect the members' welfare from the imperfect market competition. For such purposes, we review the literature on the identification of asymmetric price transmission and the pricing policy in consumer cooperatives in Korea – specifically iCOOP. That's because farmers as producers and consumers are disadvantaged by these asymmetries if they are due to the exploitation of market power by processing industries or retail organizations (McCorriston et al., 1998; Bunte and Peerlings, 2003).

This empirical study, based on asymmetric error correction model (Meyer and von Cramon-Taubadel, 2004), finds evidence that the asymmetry of price transmission in conventional agricultural products market is considerably alleviated under the pricing policy used by iCOOP. The findings also suggest that consumer cooperatives could contribute to enhancing the welfare of producers as well as consumers by their stable pricing policy favorable to both producers and consumers. These evidences implicate that consumer cooperatives contribute to promoting a more balanced redistribution of wealth. Therefore, this research on the performance of consumer cooperatives suggests the economic role of consumer cooperatives as a member-owned business by analyzing the effects of price stability in iCOOP.

II.   Literature review

1.   *A theoretical strand of asymmetric price transmission*

Price, which is the primary mechanism by which various levels of the market are linked, is subject to a certain degree of variation because of supply and demand fluctuations. Price transmission means the process in which main input prices (i.e. prices quoted on higher market levels like wholesale or producer markets) affect output prices (i.e. prices quoted on lower market levels like retail or consumer markets). The extent of adjustment and speed with which shocks are transmitted among producer, wholesale, and retail market prices is an important factor reflecting the action of market participants at different levels (National Department of Agriculture South Africa, 2003).

In neo-classical economics, flexible prices are responsible for efficient resource allocation, and price transmission integrates markets vertically and horizontally (Meyer and von Cramon-Taubadel, 2004). It means that increases and decreases in input prices trigger appropriate changes downstream, and that resulting changes are symmetric in terms of absolute size or timing. That is, price transmission is symmetric in market pricing models. Thus, asymmetry in price transmission could mean that price doesn't work for efficient resource allocation (i.e. market inefficiency).

1) Types and effect of asymmetric price transmission

Asymmetry in the context of price transmission could be classified largely into the next two criteria. The first refers to whether it occurs in terms of the magnitude or the speed. Asymmetry with respect to the speed of price transmission leads to a temporary transfer of welfare, the size of which depends on the lag as well as the price changes and transaction volumes involved (Meyer and von Cramon-Taubadel, 2004). Asymmetry with respect to the magnitude leads to a permanent transfer of welfare, the amount of which depends only on the price changes and transaction volumes involved.

The second refers to whether price transmission leads to increases in the margin between input price and output price or leads to decreases in the margin. Generalizing Peltzman (2000), Meyer and von Cramon-Taubadel (2004) proposes that positive asymmetric transmission be defined as a set of reactions according to which any price movement that squeezes the margin (i.e. an increase in input price or a fall in output price) is transmitted more rapidly or completely than the equivalent movements that stretch the margin. Accordingly, the positive transmission could be defined to the transmission which leads to increases in the margin between input price and output price. This classification explains efficiently the direction of welfare transfers due to asymmetric price transmission between the interested market players.

2) The causes of asymmetric price transmission

Many studies have been carried out in order to investigate what causes asymmetric price transmission. The proposed causes of APT could be classified largely into two. First, most publications on APT refer to 'non-competitive market structure' as an explanation for asymmetry. Especially in agriculture, producers at the beginning and consumers at the end of the supply chain often suspect that imperfect competition in processing and retailing allows middlemen to abuse market power (Meyer and von Cramon-Taubadel, 2004; Kinnucan and Forker, 1987; Miller and Hayenga, 2001; McCorriston, 2002; Lloyd et al., 2003). Hence, it is expected that margin-squeezing increases in input prices will be transmitted more rapidly or fully than the corresponding margin-stretching price changes, and that it leads to positive transmission which increases margin (Boyd and Brorsen, 1988; Karrenbrock, 1991; Griffith and Piggot, 1994; Mohanty et al., 1995). For example, Borenstein et al. (1997) explain that the downward stickiness of retail prices for gasoline will be caused by an oligopolistic market environment that leads to positive asymmetry.

Second, another main proposed explanation is that 'adjustment costs' (or 'menu costs') will result in asymmetry. If these costs are asymmetric with respect to changes in quantities or prices, retailers of perishable products might be reluctant to raise prices not to reduce sales, which leads to negative price transmission (Ward, 1982). However, Heien (1980) argues that asymmetric price transmission could be more easily resulted in for products with a long shelf life because changing prices can be more harmful to those products due to higher time costs and losses of goodwill.

Although many studies have tried to explain the causes of asymmetric price transmission, including other causes such as price support policy, asymmetric information, and so on, they are under controversy with ambiguous and sometimes contradictory results. Meanwhile, these lots of attempts to explain the causes could show that asymmetry in price transmission is an important issue to the interested persons and that many people face that problem broadly in markets.

2. An empirical strand of asymmetric price transmission

The defining characteristics of the literature on APT and especially estimation techniques are strongly focused on agricultural markets. And many of them identified that prices are transmitted asymmetrically in agricultural or food marketing chains (von Cramon-Taubadel, 1998; Bunte and Peerlings, 2003; Miller and Hayenga, 2001; Goodwin and Holt, 1999; Azzam, 1999; Abduali, 2002). Meyer and von Cramon-Taubadel (2004) show that most of the 40 empirical studies on asymmetric price transmission which were published in major journals from 1980 to 2002 are concerned with agricultural or food distribution channels. These empirical researches suggest that changes in producer or wholesale prices are not fully or too much transmitted into consumer price. Farmers and consumers are disadvantaged by these asymmetries due to the exploitation of market power by food-processing industries or retail businesses (McCorriston et al., 1998; Bunte and Peerlings, 2003).

Even if the empirical studies show different research findings in applied econometric models, research projects of identifying asymmetric price transmission have been persistently undertaken. According to the co-integrated relationship between input price and output price, these investigations could be classified largely into two groups.[1]

Autoregressive Distributed Lag (ARDL) Model is the fundamental one in pre-cointegration approaches[2] to test for asymmetric price transmission. In an ARDL, a variable y_t, where $t = 1, \ldots, n$, depends on its own lags (autoregressive part, or AR) and on a vector of variables X, both contemporaneous and lagged (distributed lag part, or DL). If with x we indicate a single explanatory variable (i.e. an element of X), a typical ARDL can be specified as:

$$y_t = \sum_{h=1}^{r} \emptyset_h y_{t-h} + \sum_{i=0}^{s} \alpha_i x_{t-i} + \epsilon_t \qquad (1)$$

where ϵ_t is white noise. Model (1) can be generalized to incorporate asymmetries by assuming that x has a different impact on y, according to whether its sign is positive (+) or negative (−):

$$y_t = \sum_{h=1}^{r} \emptyset_h y_{t-h} + \sum_{i=0}^{s} \alpha^+_i x^+_{t-i} + \sum_{j=0}^{q} \alpha^-_j x^-_{t-j} + \epsilon_t \qquad (2)$$

(Frey and Manera, 2007). In summary, an ARDL model suggests that a present output price depends on both present and past input prices, as well as own past prices (i.e. past output prices).

Meanwhile, considering a linear combination between a pair of $I(1)$ series which is stationary, the empirical studies to draw on cointegration analyses in testing for asymmetric price transmission have been conducted.

Engle and Granger (1987) develop an equilibrium correction representation, which, given two $I(1)$ variables y and x which are cointegrated with cointegrating vector $(1 - \theta)$, can be written as follows:

$$\Delta y_t = \alpha \Delta x_t + \lambda(y_{t-1} - \theta x_{t-1}) + \epsilon_t \tag{3}$$

Lagged variables and autoregressive effects can be added to this model, which is also able to incorporate asymmetries as proposed by Granger and Lee (1989):

$$\Delta y_t = \sum_{b=1}^{r} \beta_b \Delta y_{t-b} + \sum_{i=0}^{s} \alpha_i^+ \Delta x_{t-i}^+ + \sum_{j=0}^{q} \alpha_i^- \Delta x_{t-i}^-$$
$$+ \lambda^+ ECT_{t-1}^+ + \lambda^- ECT_{t-1}^- + \epsilon_t \tag{4}$$

where $ECT_{t-1} = (y_{t-1} - \theta\, x_{t-1})$. Model (4) can also be extended as Enders and Granger (1998) suggested:

$$\Delta y_t = \sum_{i=0}^{s} \alpha_i \Delta x_{t-i} + \gamma^+ ECT_{t-1} I_t + \gamma^- ECT_{t-1} I_t + \epsilon_t \tag{5}$$

where $I_t = \begin{cases} 1 & if\ \Delta ECT_{t-1} \geq 0 \\ 0 & if\ \Delta ECT_{t-1} < 0 \end{cases}$. In this case, asymmetries arise as depending on whether the deviation from the equilibrium is increasing or decreasing. These asymmetries are known as momentum equilibrium adjustment path asymmetries (MEAPA; Frey and Manera, 2007).

In short, an ECM model devises that a present output price depends, like in an ARDL model, on both present and past input prices, as well as own past prices (i.e. past output prices), and additionally depends on a long-term relationship between output prices and input prices. Most of all, an ECM model considers all the asymmetries which are testable within the ARDL specification and also supports a test for symmetric equilibrium adjustment path. If $\lambda^+ \neq \lambda^-$, the convergence process is different depending on the direction of the deviation from the equilibrium level (Frey and Manera, 2007).

III.   Pricing policy of consumer cooperatives

1.   *Pricing system based on contract farming with direct transaction*

Consumer cooperatives in Korea, including iCOOP, carry out the direct transactions of eco-friendly and organic agricultural products through contract farming. Their pricing policies are based on the direct transactions and are designed fundamentally not for profit. Such pricing policies are divided into two categories according to the classification of the direct transactions of those agricultural products. One is the fixed-pricing policy, and the other is the flexible-pricing policy.

1) Fixed pricing policy

Fixed pricing policy is carried out in 'Direct Distribution',[3] which is the general transaction system in consumer cooperatives in Korea. In this general system, producers sell their products to consumer cooperatives at the price which is set in contract with consumer cooperatives before farming. And a consumer price is set to agreed-upon price, being added basic operational costs. However, this policy fails to balance out supply and demand or absorb shocks in markets, although it keeps consumer prices stable. It's because consumer cooperatives can't force producers to supply their products to cooperatives, even when market prices are higher than the producer price in cooperatives. With producers, consumer cooperatives make a contract only for the producer price, not the quantity to supply.

Table 4.1 Two pricing policies by the ways to conduct the direct transactions

	Fixed pricing policy ('Direct distribution') (before 2010)	Flexible pricing policy ('Sales agency' in iCOOP)
Contract object	Price	Supply quantity (sales volume)
Concept	Guarantees the price of agricultural products	Guarantees producers' income (creating additional income through investment in primary production and processing)
Supply quantity	Not set in the contract	Producers are responsible for providing the entire supply quantity (130–200% of expected consumption)
Producer price	Maintaining a set price to guarantee production costs	Basic price (i.e. guaranteed production cost) and a target price (i.e. variable price)
Price fluctuation	Consumer price is set to agreed-upon price	Variable price (flexible managing in accordance with changing the market price and member demands)
Characteristics	Cannot balance out supply and demand or absorb shocks in the market	Securing stable supply quantity and having a flexible pricing system to meet supply and demand

Sources: Revised on Shin (2011), Jeong et al. (2011), and Kim (2013).

Notes: In harmony with this flexible policy, iCOOP carries out 'pre-purchase of domestic grain fund' and 'price stabilization fund' for protection from damage due to poor sales or loss of potential profits from increased market prices. And all of them function together as a stability mechanism.

2) Flexible pricing policy

Flexible pricing policy is a unique policy which is carried out in 'Sales Agency'[4] of iCOOP. iCOOP devised a new pricing policy to achieve a stable supply at a stable and reasonable price. The most distinct difference from the fixed pricing policy is the producers are required to be a member of iCOOP Association of Producer Groups and commit to providing an agreed-upon amount on a contract. That is, the policy guarantees producers a reasonable income[5] while providing consumers with eco-friendly and organic agricultural products at a cheaper and more stable year-round price than commercial enterprises (Kim, 2013). For this purpose, iCOOP is responsible for selling or processing the full amount and determines consumer prices based on the harvest, changes in demand, and fluctuating market prices. Additionally, the functioning as stability mechanism is complemented with 'Price Stabilization Fund'[6] and 'Pre-purchase of domestic grain fund'.[7]

2. The possibility of mitigating asymmetry in consumer cooperatives: research question

In a typical industry market, we commonly observe asymmetric price transmission, which is regarded as indirect evidence of imperfect competition and is intensified in the market where the distribution process is long and complex. Farmers as producers and consumers are disadvantaged by these asymmetries

Table 4.2 The stability mechanism of flexible pricing policy in iCOOP

Three elements	Operation characteristics
Flexible pricing system	A basic and target price are set; when the selling price drops and the basic income of producers aren't secured, iCOOP injects the price stabilization fund and deposits the damage.
	• Basic price: the sum of the cash costs of production – such as the cost of seeds, labor (excluding the farmer's own labor), and other inputs – and an additional 10%–20%. iCOOP guarantees this price whether or not the sales target is achieved.
	• Target price: a standard price used to decide the administration of price stabilization fund. When a product is sold at higher than this price, 20%–30% of the difference is placed into the price stabilization fund. The target and basic price are decided every year by iCOOP's Association of Producer Groups.
Advance payment	At the beginning of production, iCOOP pays 10%–15% of the basic price within the sale agency system to the producers.
Producer's income	Producer's income = [selling price – production cost (i.e. the producer's commission)] ± (price stabilization fund saving or payment)

Sources: Revised on Shin (2011), Jeong et al. (2011), and Kim (2013).

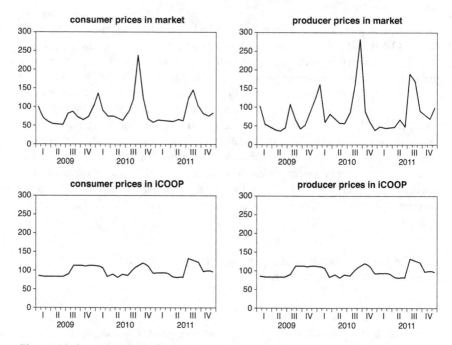

Figure 4.1 A comparison of prices in market and iCOOP (lettuce)

due to the exploitation of market power by processing industries or retail organizations (McCorriston et al., 1998; Bunte and Peerlings, 2003).

As a consumer cooperative, which could play an important role even in sustaining the economic benefits of their members from their businesses, iCOOP would present a case to show the possibility of an effective pricing system for the economic benefits of the persons interested. That's because pricing policies in consumer cooperatives in Korea are based on direct transactions and devised to keep the selling prices to consumers stable. Especially, iCOOP has revised the pricing system of agricultural products to guarantee producers a reasonable income while providing consumers with their products at a reasonable and stable price. And it was designed to sustain the economic benefits for their members and also for producers, who are the counterpart in contract farming. With such pricing policies, iCOOP seeks to maintain the agricultural products price stable and to integrate the interests of producers into those of consumers.

Therefore, with these pricing policies, consumer cooperatives in Korea could face the less likelihood of asymmetric price transmission by easing price volatility and by integrating the interests of consumers and producers, especially in iCOOP. Thus, it is expected that asymmetries are mitigated in such a pricing system in consumer cooperatives, specifically iCOOP.

IV. Methodology

1. Hypothesis and research model

This chapter aims to investigate whether the pricing policy of consumer coopera-tives mitigates the degree of asymmetric price transmission in agricultural prod-ucts markets. Furthermore, we examine how consumer cooperatives could protect the consumers' welfare from the imperfect market competition. Therefore, we analyze the vertical price transmission between producer and consumer prices for several goods in iCOOP (called 'co-op model') and compare the asymmetries with those in agricultural products market (called 'market model') for the same products, respectively. Accordingly, we need to test the asymmetries both in the markets and iCOOP, using the specific econometric model and hypotheses as follows.

In line with most studies based on extended Error Correction Models, according to Engle and Granger (1987), and Granger and Lee (1989), we assume that producer prices lead consumer prices (Kinnucan and Forker, 1987; Boyd and Brorsen, 1988; Pick et al., 1990; Griffith and Piggot, 1994; Powers, 1995). The specification of the ECM with symmetric adjustment to deviations from the long-term equilibrium is given in equation (6) and (7).

$$p_t^r = \phi_0 + \phi_1 p_t^f + \varepsilon_t \tag{6}$$

$$\Delta p_t^r = \gamma + \sum_{i=1}^{n} \alpha_i \Delta p_{t-i}^r + \sum_{j=0}^{n} \beta_j \Delta p_{t-j}^f + \lambda ECT_{t-1} + \varepsilon_t \tag{7}$$

where the superscripts r and f indicate consumer and producer prices, respec-tively. The lagged residuals from (6) are then used as the error correction term (ECT) to estimate (7).[8] λ measures adjustments to deviations from the long-term equilibrium, while short-term dynamics are measured by the α_i and β_j coeffi-cients. To allow for asymmetric price adjustment, we also estimate the ECM in (7) in which the ECT is segmented into positive (ECT^+) and negative (ECT^-) deviations from the long-term equilibrium (von Cramon-Taubadel, 1998). Asymmetry is concluded if λ^+ differs significantly from λ^-. Then, the research model based on ECM (8) shows us all the asymmetries which are testable within the ARDL specification, and also supports a test for symmetric equilibrium adjustment path.[9]

$$\Delta p_t^r = \gamma + \sum_{i=1}^{n} \alpha_i^+ \Delta p_{t-i}^r D^+ + \sum_{i=1}^{n} \alpha_i^- \Delta p_{t-i}^r D^-$$

$$+ \sum_{j=0}^{n} \beta_j^+ \Delta p_{t-j}^f D^+ + \sum_{j=0}^{n} \beta_j^- \Delta p_{t-j}^f D^-$$

$$+ \lambda^+ ECT_{t-1}^+ + \lambda^- ECT_{t-1}^- + \epsilon_t \tag{8}$$

where

$$D^+ = \begin{cases} 1 & \textit{if } \Delta p^r_{t-i} \geq 0 \textit{ or } \Delta p^f_{t-j} \geq 0 \\ 0 & \textit{otherwise} \end{cases},$$

$$D^- = \begin{cases} 1 & \textit{if } \Delta p^r_{t-i} < 0 \textit{ or } \Delta p^f_{t-j} < 0 \\ 0 & \textit{otherwise} \end{cases},$$

and $\mathrm{ECT}_{t-1} = ECT^+_{t-1} + ECT^-_{t-1} = \varepsilon_{t-1} = p^r_{t-1} - \phi_0 - \phi_1 p^f_{t-1}.$

The testing hypotheses are as follows. We could demonstrate all the asymmetries which are testable within the ARDL specification – contemporaneous impact lagged effect and cumulated impact, and long-term equilibrium adjustment effect, respectively.

$$H_0^{\text{con.}} : \beta_0^+ = \beta_0^- \tag{9}$$

$$H_0^{\text{D.L.}} : \beta_j^+ = \beta_j^- \qquad (j = 1, \cdots, n) \tag{10}$$

$$H_0^{\text{cum.}} : \sum_{j=0}^n \beta_j^+ = \sum_{j=0}^n \beta_j^- \tag{11}$$

$$H_0^{\text{adj.}} : \lambda^+ = \lambda^- \tag{12}$$

2. Research design

1) Research instrument

We analyze the vertical price transmission between producer and consumer prices for several goods in iCOOP, and compare the asymmetries with those in agricultural products market for the same products, respectively. We conduct our analysis using monthly prices between January 2008 and December 2012 (60 months) for nine products – potato, hot pepper, garlic, mushroom, lettuce, onion, cucumber, and green pepper – in both markets and iCOOP. In markets, we have information on prices both at the wholesale and at the retail level collected by Statistics Korea, such as producer price index and consumer price index for each product (Shim et al., 2006; Ahn, 2007; Kang, 2007; Ahn and Kim, 2008; Kim and Ahn, 2010). In iCOOP, we collected the prices which iCOOP pays to producers and the selling prices to iCOOP members, for each product respectively. And we had the raw data standardized according to the criteria of the price index,[10] and generated producer and consumer indices for each product.

2) *Analytical method*

We first test all producer and consumer price indices in both markets and iCOOP for a unit-root using augmented Dickey-Fuller (1981; ADF) tests. The tests confirm that, in iCOOP, both producer price and the consumer price series for three products (garlic, mushroom, lettuce) are I(1), and both price series for garlic in the market also are I(1). Additionally, the products for which one of those series is I(1) in iCOOP are three (potato, hot pepper, onion), and in the market are none. For the I(1) series, the tests for cointegration (Johansen, 1988) confirm that both price series are cointegrated except garlic in market and iCOOP, and mushroom in iCOOP. We, therefore, use an error correction model (ECM) to estimate price transmission between producer and consumer price series, for the products which were confirmed to be cointegrated. We also use an ARDL model for the rest which was not cointegrated, as like for the products which both prices are found to be stationary.[11]

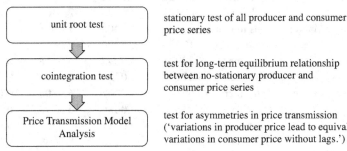

Figure 4.2 Analysis process

Table 4.3 Applied analysis model for each case

Product	Market model	Co-op model
Potato	ARDL	ECM
Hot pepper	ARDL	ECM
Garlic	ARDL	ARDL
Mushroom	ARDL	ARDL
Lettuce	ARDL	ECM
Onion	ARDL	ECM
Cucumber	ARDL	ARDL
Tomato	ARDL	ARDL
Green pepper	ARDL	ARDL

Table 4.4 Unit Rood test (ADF-test)

Product	Price series		Level		Difference	
			Test statistics	P-value	Test statistics	P-value
Potato	Market	Consumer	−4.6515	0.0004	−5.8644	0.0000
		Producer	−4.8253	0.0013	−7.0352	0.0000
	Co-op.	Consumer	−3.8662	0.0199	−6.3512	0.0000
		Producer	−4.3144	0.0010	−8.6190	0.0000
Hot pepper	Market	Consumer	−5.2003	0.0004	−6.4535	0.0000
		Producer	−4.3231	0.0010	−7.3598	0.0000
	Co-op.	Consumer	−6.4534	0.0000	−7.5550	0.0000
		Producer	−2.0285	0.2741	−6.8409	0.0000
Garlic	Market	Consumer	−2.0506	0.5617	−3.7032	0.0004
		Producer	−1.9135	0.6348	−4.7622	0.0000
	Co-op.	Consumer	−2.1757	0.4938	−6.3193	0.0000
		Producer	−3.1419	0.1065	−7.1558	0.0000
Mushroom	Market	Consumer	−4.8464	0.0012	−10.3498	0.0000
		Producer	−5.8112	0.0000	−10.8521	0.0000
	Co-op.	Consumer	−2.9111	0.1666	−9.5460	0.0000
		Producer	−2.0369	0.5693	−7.3467	0.0000
Lettuce	Market	Consumer	−5.3013	0.0003	−8.4081	0.0000
		Producer	−5.1780	0.0004	−9.0523	0.0000
	Co-op.	Consumer	−3.3397	0.0699	−6.6613	0.0000
		Producer	−3.8116	0.0227	−7.2787	0.0000
Onion	Market	Consumer	−3.6914	0.0067	−6.0808	0.0000
		Producer	−3.9685	0.0030	−6.7993	0.0000
	Co-op.	Consumer	−4.8914	0.0011	−7.2393	0.0000
		Producer	−3.9340	0.0166	−8.3039	0.0000
Cucumber	Market	Consumer	−4.9609	0.0008	−7.0481	0.0000
		Producer	−6.3580	0.0000	−5.4631	0.0000
	Co-op.	Consumer	−5.8144	0.0001	−6.5272	0.0000
		Producer	−4.2614	0.0068	−8.6102	0.0000
Tomato	Market	Consumer	−5.6726	0.0001	−6.8667	0.0000
		Producer	−4.9969	0.0008	−6.4084	0.0000
	Co-op.	Consumer	−4.8057	0.0014	−5.2926	0.0000
		Producer	−4.7703	0.0016	−9.5613	0.0000
Green pepper	Market	Consumer	−5.3029	0.0003	−6.6958	0.0000
		Producer	−4.5538	0.0005	−4.7840	0.0003
	Co-op.	Consumer	−4.9549	0.0009	−6.0294	0.0000
		Producer	−4.1393	0.0018	−5.9933	0.0000

Table 4.5 Cointegration test (Johansen test)

Product	Model	No. Of ce(s)	Hypothesized no. of ce(s)[1]	Trace-statistics (lr)	5% trace	P-value
Potato	Co-op.	2	None*	38.3420	20.2618	0.0001
			At most 1*	14.1685	9.1645	0.0053
Hot pepper	Co-op.	2	None*	45.0025	20.2618	0.0000
			At most 1*	16.1562	9.1645	0.0021
Garlic	Market	0	None	9.9990	15.4947	0.2808
			At most 1	2.2440	3.8415	0.1341
	Co-op.	0	None	15.2804	15.4947	0.0538
			At most 1	2.0862	3.8415	0.1486
Mushroom	Co-op.	0	None	10.1204	15.4947	0.2716
			At most 1	1.2307	3.8415	0.2673
Lettuce	Co-op.	1	None*	19.4715	15.4947	0.0119
			At most 1	3.6026	3.8415	0.0577
Onion	Co-op.	2	None*	30.8895	15.4947	0.0001
			At most 1*	9.8198	3.8415	0.0017

Note: * indicates being significant at 5% of a significance level.

V. Empirical results

Farmers and consumers are disadvantaged by the asymmetries in price transmission due to the exploitation of market power by processing industries or retail organizations (McCorriston et al., 1998; Bunte and Peerlings, 2003). Such asymmetries could represent welfare transfer from farmer or consumer to processing industries or retail organizations.

In order to investigate whether consumer cooperatives mitigate the asymmetries occurred in markets, we need to compare the asymmetries in typical agricultural product markets with as those in consumer cooperatives, specifically iCOOP. Therefore, we analyze the vertical price transmission between producer and consumer prices for agricultural products in iCOOP and compare the asymmetries with those in agricultural product markets by product, respectively. Accordingly, we need to test the asymmetries both in markets and iCOOP, using the specific model and hypotheses.

1. Price transmission model estimation

We estimated the price transmission model that variations in producer price series are transmitted to consumer price series, for both models (market and co-op). In the estimation by case, the lag-lengths n is determined by the Akaike Information Criteria (AIC) and the Schwartz Criteria (SC). In any model, a trend is not found to have a significant impact on the price transmission process for all products.[12] The goodness of fit for our price transmission model was tested with R^2. R^2, the coefficient of determination for the endogenous variables, is around 0.7 in most cases, and our model fits well for explaining the price transmission from variations in producer prices to consumer prices. The Durbin-Watson (DW) test doesn't fail to reject the null hypothesis of no autocorrelation in (8). Estimated coefficients of the price adjustment processes for nine products are presented in Tables 4.7 and 4.8, respectively.

The results given in Tables 4.2 and 4.3 reveal that there are large differences between price transmission coefficients estimated in the market model on the one hand and co-op model on the other. The most pronounced differences are found for the coefficients β_1^+ and β_0^-. Estimating the market models, contemporaneous change coefficients in positive variations (β_0^+) are statistically significant for all nine products, and the first lag effects (β_1^+), except only one product (potato), are also very significant. Additionally, this impact lasts several months. This indicates that, in the market, consumer prices react completely within one month to the producer price increase, and such impacts are inclined to last about several periods.

Also in estimating the co-op models, contemporaneous change coefficients in positive variations (β_0^+) are statistically significant for all 8 products except one (garlic). However, the impacts last to the next term (β_1^+) only in the two products (lettuce, cucumber). Thus, in consumer cooperatives, though consumer prices react contemporaneously to producer price increases, such variations couldn't lead to consumer price changes in the next month.

Additionally, in the case of producer price decreases, co-op models show that consumer prices decrease completely within the same period (β_0^-) for all nine products. In contrast, market models show that only for one product (onion), consumer prices decrease within the same period and that the impact doesn't last on. Besides, producer price decreases don't lead to consumer price decreases even with lags in marker models.

In summary, the increases in producer prices which shrank the distribution margin are transmitted more rapidly or completely than the equivalent movements that stretch the margin in the market. Such asymmetric transmission consequently leads to increases in the margin (i.e. positive transmission). In the co-op model, the decreases in producer prices which stretch the distribution margin are transmitted more rapidly or completely than the equivalent movements that squeeze the margin in the market, and it could lead to decreases in the margin (i.e. negative transmission). Therefore, this co-op model shows that consumer cooperatives could protect producers as well as consumers from the middlemen's profitable welfare transfer, rather than consumers and producers.

2. *Testing research hypotheses*

Using a Wald test, we found that symmetry can be rejected in equations (9)–(12) for many more products in the market model than in the co-op model. The result in Tables 4.8 and 4.9 shows that asymmetric price transmission is inclined

Table 4.6 Price transmission model estimation: market model

Item	Potato	Hot pepper	Garlic	Mushroom	Lettuce	Onion	Cucumber	Tomato	Green pepper
Constant	-0.09 (-0.02)	-4.98 (-2.10**)	-0.75 (-1.19)	0.46 (0.56)	-3.98 (-1.81*)	0.12 (0.08)	-13.31 (-2.19**)	-5.66 (-2.09**)	-3.18 (-1.15)
α_1^+	0.64 (2.65**)	-1.47 (-7.66***)	-0.14 (-0.68)	-1.10 (-5.39***)	-1.93 (-12.15***)	-0.77 (-3.85***)	-0.88 (-3.52***)	-0.28 (-1.05)	-1.08 (-5.24***)
α_2^+	-0.05 (-0.19)		-0.13 (-0.63)	0.67 (2.47**)		0.08 (0.35)	-0.56 (-1.99*)	-0.72 (-2.81***)	-0.98 (-0.98)
α_3^+	0.56 (2.03*)		-0.20 (-1.04)				0.29 (1.09)	-0.70 (-3.18***)	-0.98 (-4.94***)
α_4^+	-0.42 (-1.60)						-0.74 (-2.23**)		
α_5^+	-0.90 (-3.45***)						-0.51 (-1.52)		
α_1^-	0.24 (1.05)	0.31 (2.71***)	0.15 (0.65)	0.56 (2.50**)	0.34 (4.78***)	0.50 (2.59**)	-0.04 (-0.15)	0.17 (0.95)	0.15 (1.15)
α_2^-	-0.04 (-0.18)		-0.23 (-0.92)	0.24 (1.57)		0.00 (-0.02)	0.53 (2.01**)	-0.07 (-0.41)	0.10 (0.70)
α_3^-	-0.18 (-0.82)		0.79 (3.31***)				-0.08 (-0.34)	0.18 (0.98)	
α_4^-	0.01 (0.09)						0.03 (0.11)		
α_5^-	-0.29 (-1.64)						-0.38 (-1.72*)		
β_0^+	0.40 (4.17***)	0.63 (8.32***)	0.53 (7.08***)	0.27 (5.73***)	0.66 (13.26***)	0.49 (5.58***)	0.82 (4.88***)	0.90 (9.07***)	0.51 (8.30***)
β_1^+	-0.09 (-0.82)	0.91 (7.75***)	0.37 (3.17***)	0.17 (2.58**)	1.00 (8.40***)	0.68 (4.45***)	0.71 (3.78***)	0.45 (2.44**)	0.71 (6.50***)

(Continued)

Table 4.6 (Continued)

Item	Potato	Hot pepper	Garlic	Mushroom	Lettuce	Onion	Cucumber	Tomato	Green pepper
β_2^+	-0.58 (-5.45***)		0.11 (0.80)	-0.18 (-2.62**)		-0.25 (-1.51)	0.27 (1.06)	0.36 (1.84*)	0.39 (2.98***)
β_3^+	-0.08 (-0.48)		0.03 (0.22)				-0.10 (-0.43)	0.45 (2.50**)	
β_4^+	0.22 (1.56)						0.61 (2.25**)		
β_5^+	0.13 (0.88)						0.70 (2.36**)		
β_0^-	0.05 (0.39)	0.04 (0.38)	0.02 (0.41)	0.12 (0.58)	-0.10 (-0.53)	0.39 (2.77***)	0.60 (1.61)	0.45 (1.32)	-0.19 (-0.95)
β_1^-	0.00 (0.05)	-0.17 (-1.74*)	-0.08 (-1.61)	-0.06 (-0.29)	-0.21 (-1.17)	-0.10 (-0.68)	-0.48 (-1.28)	-0.28 (-0.85)	0.10 (0.55)
β_2^-	-0.10 (-0.97)		0.00 (-0.04)	-0.48 (-2.44**)		0.25 (1.75*)	-0.46 (-1.18)	0.03 (0.10)	0.04 (0.20)
β_3^-	0.11 (1.13)		-0.05 (-1.21)				-0.35 (-0.87)	0.07 (0.27)	
β_4^-	0.17 (1.65)						0.00 (0.01)		
β_5^-	-0.10 (-1.14)						-0.01 (-0.03)		
R^2	0.85	0.78	0.80	0.69	0.91	0.83	0.81	0.80	0.83
Adj. R^2	0.74	0.76	0.73	0.62	0.90	0.79	0.68	0.74	0.80
AIC	7.39	7.58	4.76	5.08	7.85	6.56	8.14	7.24	7.55
SC	8.23	7.83	5.31	5.48	8.10	6.96	8.99	7.79	7.94
DW	2.40	2.11	2.26	2.00	2.04	1.91	1.79	1.89	1.95
F-stat.	7.93	30.78	11.75	10.31	85.71	21.95	6.07	12.06	22.79
P-value	0.00	0.00	0.00	0.00	0.00	0.00	0.00	0.00	0.00

Notes: Coefficient (t-value in blank)

Table 4.7 Price transmission model estimation: co-op model

Item	Potato	Hot pepper	Garlic	Mushroom	Lettuce	Onion	Cucumber	Tomato	Green pepper
Constant	3.74 (1.27)	-4.95 (-0.74)	-0.88 (-1.01)	-0.37 (-1.88*)	-1.84 (-1.58)	3.24 (1.63)	0.05 (0.03)	0.22 (0.08)	-2.82 (-1.05)
α_1^+	0.20 (1.06)	-0.09 (-0.39)	0.50 (2.73**)	0.08 (0.82)	0.28 (2.06**)	0.09 (0.51)	-0.41 (-2.78***)	-0.32 (-1.95*)	0.06 (0.33)
α_2^+		-0.23 (-0.98)	0.39 (1.96*)				-0.18 (-1.25)	-0.45 (-2.89***)	0.02 (0.08)
α_3^+		0.09 (0.43)	-0.75 (-3.67***)					-0.02 (-0.19)	-0.23 (-1.14)
α_4^+		0.38 (2.13**)	-0.15 (-0.73)					0.03 (0.18)	
α_5^+			-0.03 (-0.19)						
α_1^-	0.02 (0.15)	-0.15 (-0.45)	-0.59 (-2.86***)	-0.70 (-2.62**)	-0.05 (-0.34)	0.03 (0.14)	-0.25 (-1.26)	0.68 (2.29**)	-0.07 (-0.33)
α_2^-		1.01 (3.23***)	0.16 (0.80)				0.06 (0.29)	0.28 (0.74)	-0.18 (-0.82)
α_3^-		0.50 (1.53)	-0.16 (-0.80)					0.24 (0.93)	0.11 (0.49)
α_4^-		-0.02 (-0.06)	-0.31 (-1.56)					-0.22 (-0.83)	
α_5^-			-0.68 (-3.22***)						
β_0^+	0.44 (3.74***)	0.67 (4.53***)	-0.01 (-0.16)	0.58 (5.36***)	0.36 (3.33***)	-0.15 (-1.71*)	0.92 (7.67***)	1.34 (6.06***)	0.51 (3.38***)

(Continued)

Table 4.7 (Continued)

Item	Potato	Hot pepper	Garlic	Mushroom	Lettuce	Onion	Cucumber	Tomato	Green pepper
β_1^+	0.01	0.42	-0.11	0.11	0.27	0.15	0.48	0.58	0.25
	(0.11)	(1.97*)	(-1.55)	(0.89)	(2.31**)	(1.40)	(3.02***)	(1.62)	(1.59)
β_2^+		0.16	0.01				0.14	0.84	0.32
		(0.70)	(0.10)				(0.87)	(2.61**)	(1.97*)
β_3^+		0.37	0.00					0.38	0.61
		(1.51)	(0.07)					(1.57)	(3.25***)
β_4^+		0.13	-0.02					0.08	
		(0.61)	(-0.34)					(0.27)	
β_5^+			-0.22						
			(-2.46**)						
β_0^-	0.82	0.58	1.01	1.06	0.87	0.94	1.03	0.94	0.83
	(6.70***)	(3.11***)	(9.92***)	(11.92***)	(11.78***)	(8.35***)	(17.45***)	(10.39***)	(5.80***)
β_1^-	0.10	0.00	-0.04	0.21	-0.03	0.19	0.23	-0.68	-0.01
	(0.55)	(0.02)	(-0.23)	(0.89)	(-0.22)	(1.02)	(1.36)	(-2.61**)	(-0.06)
β_2^-		-1.01	-0.49				0.08	-0.21	0.20
		(-3.51***)	(-2.48**)				(0.49)	(-0.61)	(0.90)
β_3^-		-0.58	0.34					-0.40	-0.08
		(-1.80*)	(1.79*)					(-1.66)	(-0.35)
β_4^-		-0.06	0.26					0.04	
		(-0.21)	(1.27)					(0.15)	
β_5^-			0.09						
			(0.50)						

λ^+	-0.67	-0.58		-0.20	-0.19			
	(-5.03***)	(-2.32**)		(-2.20**)	(-1.46)			
λ^-	0.18	-0.03		-0.14	0.05			
	(0.92)	(-0.16)		(-1.54)	(0.36)			
R^2	0.73	0.88	0.84	0.87	0.72	0.92	0.91	0.73
adj. R^2	0.68	0.79	0.82	0.84	0.68	0.90	0.86	0.63
AIC	7.64	5.40	2.93	5.97	7.04	6.34	6.42	7.14
SC	7.96	6.25	3.18	6.28	7.36	6.74	7.12	7.69
DW	1.91	2.02	1.91	2.17	1.89	2.06	1.85	2.09
F-stat.	16.25	9.96	44.81	39.83	16.14	51.78	19.46	7.80
P-value	0.00	0.00	0.00	0.00	0.00	0.00	0.00	0.00

Notes: Coefficient (t-value in blank)

*** (**, *) indicates being significant at 1 (5, 10) % of a significance level.

Table 4.8 Price transmission hypothesis test

Item		Market model				Co-op model			
		(a) Con.	(b) D.l.	(c) Cum.	(d) Adj.	(a) Con.	(b) D.l.	(c) Cum.	(d) Adj.
Potato	F-statistic	5.18**	3.31**	0.14		4.29**	0.16	3.04	9.24***
	P-value	0.03	0.02	0.71		0.04	0.69	0.09	0.00
Hot pepper	F-statistic	22.31***	57.36***	76.76***		0.10	4.22***	8.04***	3.11
	P-value	0.00	0.00	0.00		0.76	0.01	0.01	0.09
Garlic	F-statistic	35.73***	4.16**	13.78***		77.29***	2.19	12.22***	
	P-value	0.00	0.01	0.00		0.00	0.08	0.00	
Mushroom	F-statistic	0.56	1.64	3.14		9.68***	0.16	3.60	
	P-value	0.46	0.21	0.08		0.00	0.69	0.06	
Lettuce	F-statistic	14.94***	33.05***	37.35***		13.79***	3.93	0.79	0.12
	P-value	0.00	0.00	0.00		0.00	0.05	0.38	0.73
Onion	F-statistic	0.26	6.29***	1.49		56.87***	0.03	15.34***	1.14
	P-value	0.61	0.00	0.23		0.00	0.87	0.00	0.29
Cucumber	F-statistic	0.28	2.20	7.98***		0.65	1.51	0.49	
	P-value	0.60	0.08	0.01		0.42	0.23	0.49	
Tomato	F-statistic	1.54	2.15	6.43**		2.45	4.00***	10.81***	
	P-value	0.22	0.11	0.02		0.13	0.01	0.00	
Green pepper	F-statistic	11.84***	5.24***	17.38***		2.13	1.92	1.48	
	P-value	0.00	0.01	0.00		0.15	0.14	0.23	

Notes: *** (**) indicates being significant at 1 (5)% of a significance level.

(A) CON. = contemporaneous effect, (B) D.L. = distributed lags effect, (C) CUM. = cumulative effect, (D) ADJ. = adjustment effect

Table 4.9 Asymmetric price transmission products in each effect

Market model				Co-op model			
(A) CON.	*(B)* D.L.	*(C)* CUM.	*(D)** ADJ.	*(A)* CON.	*(B)* D.L.	*(C)* CUM.	*(D)* ADJ.
Potato	Potato	Hot pepper	•	Potato	Hot pepper	Hot pepper	Potato
Hot pepper	Hot pepper	Garlic		Garlic	Tomato	Garlic	
Garlic	Garlic	Lettuce		Mushroom		Onion	
Lettuce	Lettuce	Cucumber		Lettuce		Tomato	
Green pepper	Onion	Tomato		Onion			
	Green pepper	Green pepper					

Note: Testing market models are based on an ARDL model. Thus, there are no products to test adjustment effect.

to occur for many more products in the market. The most distinct differences are found for the lagged effect[13] and the cumulative impact[14] in equation (10) and (11), respectively. Variations in producer price in the past periods are asymmetrically transmitted to consumer price with lags for six products in market model, while they are only for two products.

Additionally, in the effect which, being cumulated, those variations in several past periods impact on current consumer price, asymmetries grow more and more involved in the market model. Contemporaneous asymmetries[15] are found for five products in the market, while lagged and cumulative asymmetries are for six products. In contrast, lagged and cumulative asymmetries are found for two and four products, respectively, though contemporaneous asymmetries are for five products in the co-op model.

VI. Conclusion

Consumer cooperatives could play an important role even in sustaining the economic benefits of their members from their businesses. The purpose of the pricing system of agricultural products in consumer cooperatives could be to build a sustainable structure of food production and consumption. This is achieved by transforming a market-based antagonistic relationship between producers (seeking to sell at the highest price possible) and consumers (seeking to buy at the lowest price possible) to a win-win cooperative price system based on mutual trust and cooperation with common interests. With these pricing policies, consumer cooperatives in Korea could face the less likelihood of asymmetric price transmission by easing price volatility and by integrating the interests of consumers and producers, especially in iCOOP. Thus, it is expected that asymmetries are mitigated in such a pricing system in consumer cooperatives, specifically iCOOP.

This empirical study finds the asymmetry of price transmission in conventional agricultural products market is considerably alleviated under the pricing policy used by consumer cooperatives, specifically iCOOP. The findings also suggest that consumer cooperatives could contribute to enhancing the welfare of producers as well as consumers by their stable pricing policy favorable to both producers and consumers. These implicate consumer cooperatives contribute to promoting a more balanced redistribution of wealth. Therefore, this research on the performance of consumer cooperatives suggests the economic role of consumer cooperatives as a member-owned business by analyzing the effects of price stability in iCOOP.

Notes

1 Granger and Newbold (1974) demonstrate that regressing involving non-stationary variables (or variables that display similar behavior) often produce results that are spuriously significant, suggesting the existence of relationships that do not, in fact, exist. Engle and Granger (1987) point out that, given a pair of I(1) series, if there exists a linear combination between them which is stationary, the two processes move together in the LR and are said to be cointegrated. In analyzing with non-stationary time series variables, cointegration analysis helps us to find an appropriate econometric method with which we can interpret regression results properly and meaningfully.

2 These approaches are not interested in the stationary of times series variables (i.e. input prices and output prices) or don't have to be interested in it because those variables are stationary.

3 In a direct distribution system in consumer cooperatives in Korea, agricultural products follow the simple distribution process from producers to consumers. The agricultural products are delivered through a supply chain which has so simple steps (i.e. *'producers → consumer co-operative → consumers'*).

4 In this system, agricultural products are delivered through the simple supply chain, as like in the Direct Distribution system (i.e. 'producers – a consumer cooperative – consumers').

5 According to the survey asked iCOOP's 25 partner producers, the money they received after the implementation of the sale agency-flexible pricing system was 66%–73% of the selling price to consumers. This was higher than the money received by the typical farmer, 60% of the selling price to consumers (Kim, 2013).

6 iCOOP operates PSF to guarantee a producer's income when the market price of agricultural products falls sharply. Producers, processing producers, and consumers join to raise funds as follows: producers are saving 20%–30% of the difference when an agricultural product is sold at higher than the target price; processing producers (food manufacturer) are saving 0.9% of total delivery price; and consumers are saving 500 won (0.5 dollar)/month per person. This fund stabilizes prices for consumers and producers when the price of agricultural products increases sharply or when they plummet. Thus, both consumers and producers are guaranteed a stable, just, and sustainable price. The benefits of this mechanism have attracted great attention especially from the government and media. In 2012, the fund raised 5 billion won (5 million dollars) and spent 2.5 billion won (2.5 million dollars). An increase in 23% (compared to 2011) used to help producers secure a reasonable income (Kim, 2013).

7 In this system, a member-consumer pays for a product before receiving it. Production is stabilized and needed money is available for producers when beginning cultivation or harvesting. This mechanism reduces the amount of outstanding on-line accounts and also reduces credit card fees since it bypasses the use of a credit card. As of December 31, 2012, the amounts of the fund reached 25 billion won (25 million dollars; Kim, 2013).

8 In the case of no cointegration, we conduct analysis based on an ARDL model such as (7');

$$\Delta p_t^r = \gamma + \sum_{i=1}^{n} \alpha_i \Delta p_{t-i}^r + \sum_{j=0}^{n} \beta_j \Delta p_{t-j}^f + \varepsilon_t \qquad (7')$$

9 Equation (7) makes this study for testing asymmetries significant also when consumer and producer price series are not stationary (i.e. $I(1)$) or not cointegrated. Because (7) in itself is also the equation of the first difference variables, it could be statistically significant to test asymmetries using the model (8) without error correction terms. It is an ARDL model such like (7). Thus, the model (8) makes very inclusive analyzing possible, nearly regardless of the stationary state.

10 Using price indices, as like using prices itself, can make us analyze the price transmission. However, the absolute values of the coefficient estimates explain nothings but relative comparison. For instance, when the absolute value is over 1, it just means that increases of consumer price are bigger than those of producer price.

11 See footnote 4. Meanwhile, we nevertheless – for purposes of comparability – might also use an ECM in all the cases.

12 We followed a two-step procedure of Engle and Granger (1987): (1) estimate the equilibrium relation and test for cointegration; (2) estimate the ECM – that is, a regression where all variables are expressed in first differences, apart from the stationary residuals from step (1).

13 $H_0^{\text{D.L.}} : \beta_j^+ = \beta_j^- \qquad (j = 1, \cdots, n)$

14 $H_0^{\text{cum.}} : \sum_{j=0}^{n} \beta_j^+ = \sum_{j=0}^{n} \beta_j^-$

15 $H_0^{\text{con.}} : \beta_0^+ = \beta_0^-$

References

Abduali, A. (2002) 'Using Threshold Co-Integration to Estimate Asymmetric Price Transmission: In the Swiss Pork Market.' *Applied Economics*, 34: 679–687.

Ahn, B. I. (2007) 'Maneulgwa yangpae daehan gagyeokjeoniui bidaechingseong geomjeong' [Test of Asymmetric Price Transmission for Garlic and Onion]. *Journal of Rural Development*, 30(3): 51–67.

Ahn, B. I, and Kim, T. H. (2008) 'Juyo nongsanmurui saengsanjawa sobija gagyeokganui bidaechingjeok gagyeokjeoni bunseok' [Test for Asymmetric Price Transmission Between Producer and Consumer Prices of Major Agricultural Products]. *Korean Journal of Agricultural Economics*, 49(3): 77–95.

Azzam, A. M. (1999) 'Asymmetry and Rigidity in Farm-Retail Price Transmission.' *American Journal of Agricultural Economics*, 81: 525–533.

Borenstein, S., Cameron, A. C., and Gilbert, R. (1997) 'Do Gasoline Prices Respond Asymmetrically to Crude Oil Price Changes?' *The Quarterly Journal of Economics*, 112(1): 305–339.

Boyd, M. S., and Brorsen, B. W. (1988) 'Price Asymmetry in the U.S. Pork Marketing Channel.' *North Central Journal of Agricultural Economics*, 10(1): 103–109.

Bunte, F., and Peerlings, J. (2003) 'Asymmetric Price Transmission Due to Market Power in the Case of Supply Shocks.' *Agribusiness*, 19(1): 19–28.

Choi, E. J., Choi, W., Jang, S., and Park, S. (2014) 'Does the Effectiveness of Board of Directors Affect Firm Performance of Consumer Cooperatives? The Case of iCOOP KOREA.' *Annals of Public and Cooperative Economics*, 85: 371–386.

Enders, W., and Granger, C. W. J. (1998) 'Unit-Root Tests and Asymmetric Adjustment With an Example Using the Term Structure of Interest Rates.' *Journal of Business and Economic Statistics*, 16: 304–311.

Engle, R. E., and Granger, C. W. J. (1987) 'Co-Integration and Error-Correction: Representation, Estimation, and Testing.' *Econometrica*, 55: 251–276.

Frey, G., and Manera, M. (2007) 'Econometric Models of Asymmetric Price Transmission.' *Journal of Economic Surveys*, 21(2): 349–415.

Goodwin, B. K., and Holt, M. T. (1999) 'Asymmetric Adjustment and Price Transmission in the U. S. Beef Sector.' *American Journal of Agricultural Economics*, 81: 630–637.

Granger, C. W. J., and Lee, T. H. (1989) 'Investigation on Production Sales and Inventory Relationship Using Multi Co-Integration and Non-Symmetric Error Correction Models.' *Journal of Applied Econometrics*, 4: 145–159.

Granger, C. W. J., and Newbold, P. (1974) 'Spurious Regressions in Econometrics.' *Journal of Econometrics*, 22: 111–120.

Griffith, G. R., and Piggot, N. E. (1994) 'Asymmetry in Beef, Lamb and Pork Farm-Retail Price Transmission in Australia.' *Agricultural Economics*, 10: 307–316.

Heien, D. M. (1980) 'Mark Up Pricing in a Dynamic Model of Food Industry.' *American Journal of Agricultural Economics*, 62: 10–18.

Jeong, E. M. (2006) 'Hanguk saenghwalhyeopdongjohabui teukseong' [The Characteristics of Consumer Cooperatives in Korea]. *Korea Rural Economics*, 29(3): 1–18.

Jeong, E. M., Kim, D. H., and Kim, M. M. (2011) *Saenghyeop gyeongjesaeobui seonggwawa jeongchaekgwaje* [The Economic Fruits and Policy Tasks of Consumer Co-operatives in Korea]. R645, Seoul, Korea: Korea Rural Economic Institute.

Johansen, S. (1988) 'Statistical Analysis of Cointegration Vectors.' *Journal of Economic Dynamics and Control*, 12(2–3): 231–254.

Kang, T. H. (2007) 'Nongsanmurui domaegagyeokgwa somaegagyeok ganui bidaeching gagyeokjeondare gwanhan yeongu' [A Study on the Asymmetric Price Transmission Between Wholesale and Retail Agricultural Prices]. *Korean Journal of Agricultural Economics*, 48(4): 27–44.

Karrenbrock, J. D. (1991) 'The Behavior of Retail Gasoline Prices: Symmetric of Not?' *Federal Reserve Bank of St. Louis Review*, 73(4): 19–29.

Kim, H. (2013) *iCOOP KOREA's Pricing System for Sustainable Food Production and Distribution*. Paper presented at ICA International Conference 2013 ('A Co-operative Decade in Action'), Cape Town, South Africa.

Kim, T. H., and Ahn, B. I. (2010) 'Gagyeokjeoniui bidaechingseongeul iyonghan yutonggwajeongui bihyoyulseong geomjeong: nongsanmul sijangeui jeogyong' [Test for Inefficiency of the Markets for Agricultural Products Based on Asymmetric Price Transmission]. *The Korean Journal of Industrial Organization*, 18(4): 137–163.

Kinnucan, H. W., and Forker, O. D. (1987) 'Asymmetry in Farm-Retail Price Transmission for Major Dairy Products.' *American Journal of Agricultural Economics*, 69: 285–292.

Lloyd, T., McCorriston, S., Morgan, C. W., and Rayner, A. J. (2003) *The Impact of Food Scares on Price Transmission in Inter-Related Markets.* Paper presented at 15th IAAE Conference, Durban, South Africa.

McCorriston, S. (2002) 'Why Should Imperfect Competition Matter to Agricultural Economists?' *European Review of Agricultural Economics*, 29(3): 349–371.

McCorriston, S., Morgan, C. W., and Rayner, A. J. (1998) 'Processing Technology, Market Power and Price Transmission.' *Journal of Agricultural Economics*, 49(2): 185–201.

Meyer, J., and von Cramon-Taubadel, S. (2004) 'Asymmetric Price Transmission: A Survey.' *Journal of Agricultural Economics*, 55(3): 581–611.

Miller, D. J., and Hayenga, M. L. (2001) 'Price Cycles and Asymmetric Price Transmission in the U.S. Pork Market.' *American Journal of Agricultural Economics*, 83: 551–562.

Mohanty, S., Peterson, E. W. F., and Kruse, N. C. (1995) 'Price Asymmetry in the International Wheat Market.' *Canadian Journal of Agricultural Economics*, 43: 355–366.

National Department of Agriculture South Africa. (2003) 'Market Structure, Asymmetry and Price Transmission in the Food Chains.' *Food Pricing Monitoring Committee Final Report*, 5(4): 331–345.

Peltzman, S. (2000) 'Prices Rise Faster Than They Fall.' *Journal of Political Economy*, 108(3): 466–502.

Pick, D. H., Karrenbrock, J. D., and Carman, H. F. (1990) 'Price Asymmetry and Marketing Margin Behaviour: An Example for California: Arizona Citrus.' *Agribusiness*, 6(1): 75–84.

Powers, N. J. (1995) 'Sticky Short Run Prices and Vertical Pricing: Evidence From the Market for Iceberg Lettuce.' *Agribusiness*, 11: 57–75.

Shim, C., Jung, K., and Kim, M. (2006) 'Hanguk chuksanmul gagyeogui bidaechingseong' [Asymmetric Price Transmission in Korean Meat Prices]. *Korean Journal of Agricultural Management and Policy*, 33(4): 1113–1126.

Shin, S. S. (2011) *Saeroun saenghyeobundongui mirae* [The Future of Cooperatives Movement]. Seoul, Korea: Purun namu.

von Cramon-Taubadel, S. (1998) 'Estimating Asymmetric Price Transmission with the Error Correction Representation: An Application to the German Pork Market.' *European Review of Agricultural Economics*, 25: 1–18.

Ward, R. W. (1982) 'Asymmetry in Retail, Wholesale and Shipping Point Pricing for Fresh Vegetables.' *American Journal of Agricultural Economics*, 64(2): 205–212.

5 Financing consumer cooperatives

Jin-Seon Seo and Woosuk Choi

I. Introduction

Like any other business, a cooperative enterprise needs capital to do business. In the survey of the Ministry of Economy and Finance[1] in Korea, cooperatives require some of the policies to support sales for their goods (40.7%) and to support financial services (17.7%). Some cooperatives such as agricultural cooperatives and fisheries cooperatives have solved the problem of insufficient capital by being allowed to run additionally credit business in Korea. Consumer cooperatives, however, have still difficulties to finance because they cannot do credit business and have some constraint. The capital problem is a common problem from which cooperatives suffer worldwide. International Co-operative Alliance (hereafter, ICA) published 'Blueprint for A Cooperative Decade', which suggests the five agenda important for the development of cooperatives including capital (International Co-operative Alliance, 2013).

Research on the capital of cooperatives is scarce relatively not only compared to these concerns but also compared to other study subjects of cooperatives. Seo and Choi (2016) analyze the capital structure of consumer cooperatives empirically through both static trade-off and pecking order theories. They argue that both theories can explain a significant part of the capital structure of consumer cooperatives but neither of the theories seems to perfectly explain the capital structure. Choi and Seo (2014) insist that member loans make members' ownership improve and increase the patronage of members. Shim (2015) reviews the capital system for cooperatives in Korea compared to investor-owned businesses (hereafter, IOBs) from a legal perspective. In 2015, the sources of capital are investigated focusing on the largest 300 cooperatives and mutual in the world and show that cooperatives raise capital through various means such as loans, bonds and member shares (Andrews, 2015). ICA publishes a report containing meaning, philosophy, and the role which capital has in cooperatives (ICA, 2016). However, there is still a lack of academic research on the capital of cooperatives.

This chapter aims to understand why consumer cooperatives are difficult to finance, to identify necessity of member participation in funding on the basis of financial theory and to study the case of iCOOP on financing consumer cooperatives. The chapter is organized as follows: Section 2 and 3 discuss existing theories about the capital of cooperatives and previous studies on the capital of corporates in terms of information asymmetry respectively. Section 4 explains financing from members that are used for consumer cooperatives to raise capital alternatively in terms of information asymmetry. The financing of iCOOP consumer cooperatives is analyzed from this point of view in Section 5. The last section offers a summary and implications.

II.   Capital of cooperatives

It is hard for cooperatives to attract investors' interest because their purpose is not to maximize profit but to improve members' benefits. Moreover, cooperatives are based on democratic decision making, one member one vote, regardless of the amount of money invested, which is another factor making difficult to raise money from investors. It is impossible for investors to participate in the decision-making process based on the amount of investment. prior studies about the capital of cooperatives are mainly performed from this viewpoint. In the perspective of ownership, they highlight member shares or relation between the shares and the right of decision and illustrate financing through so-called innovative shares that have the attributes of IOBs. They argue that the restriction of financing of cooperative is attributed to 'vaguely defined property rights', which are characterized as non-redeemable and non-transferable shares (Cook and Iliopoulos, 1999; Chaddad and Cook, 2004; Mazzarol, 2009).

Ownership rights are separated into two distinct concepts in economic theory: residual rights of control and residual claims to assets. Residual rights of control are defined as rights to decide how the assets of a firm are used. The rights are necessary in order to minimize costs resulting from the impossibility of making, implementing and enforcing complete contracts. Shareholders must hold the right of control over the assets because they make an investment while taking risk caused by incomplete contracts among stakeholders (Grossman and Hart, 1986).

Residual claims are defined as rights to net income of a firm – that is, the rights to the residual assets after paying promised costs (e.g. wage, interest expense, raw material costs, etc.). Since net cash flows are uncertain, net income can be negative. Therefore, residual claimants are considered to hold the residual risk of a firm. The property rights theory maintains that residual claimants with residual risk are the owners of a firm (Fama and Jensen, 1983). Milgrom and Roberts (1992: 291) state that when residual claimants of a firm receive maximized value its total value will be maximized; if residual claimants have the residual right of control, they will make efficient decisions in order to pursue their own interests and maximize their own income. In other words, the value of a firm would be maximized when its residual claimants hold the residual rights of control.

Cooperatives have a limitation on dividends and member shares are generally non-appreciable and redeemable at face value only when members withdraw from cooperatives. This means a restriction on the residual claims, which affects investment and disposal over the assets. Moreover, members are those with the residual rights of control, but they cannot transfer their shares in principle. Since refund is not restricted if members leave in general and thus member might not take the risk of incomplete contracts, the residual rights of control seem to be also limited. These are the reasons why cooperatives experience difficulties of financing in the perspective of property rights theory.

Chaddad and Cook (2004: 350) define traditional cooperatives as having following attributes of ownership rights: only member-patron have ownership rights; residual claims are non-transferable, non-appreciable and redeemable; patronage refunds are distributed in proportion to patronage. They classify the types of cooperatives including recently emerging cooperatives according to the transformation of the attributes. Cooperatives are classified into seven types from traditional cooperatives to investor-oriented firms: traditional cooperatives, proportional investment cooperatives, member-investor cooperatives, new generation cooperatives, cooperatives with capital seeking entities, investor-share cooperatives, and investor-oriented firms.

However, there are limitations to explaining the difficulty of financing of cooperatives only by ownership rights. First, it cannot explicate borrowing capital such as loans. Second, it seems to be unreasonable that the property rights theory on the basis of IOBs directly applies to cooperatives owned by user-members, not investors. Furthermore, there is no empirical study whether the type of cooperatives similar to IOBs is easier to raise money up to now. Third, incorporating investors into the governance of cooperatives would be a problem. If various types of members attend the governance, the costs of decision-making could increase due to opposing interests between members (Hansmann, 1996). There are a few studies about the capital and financing of cooperatives. Most of them are based on the property rights theory, thereby the addition and transformation of member shares similar to common shares and preference shares of IOBs are mainly discussed in the funding of cooperatives (e.g. Mazzarol, 2009; Lund, 2013; Lim, 2004).

III.   Information asymmetry and corporate financing

Financial markets play a role in efficiently channelling funds from investors to firms. In an efficient capital market, funds are optimally distributed among investment opportunities, which is advantageous to both investors and firms. In addition, asset prices reflect all available relevant information fully and instantaneously (Copeland et al., 2014). Thus, stock prices in stock markets would be a signal of transferring investment information. In an efficient capital market, information which firms have is efficiently delivered to the market. Using the information investors can make decisions about investment strategies and firms are able to raise money at reasonable prices. Most studies show that capital markets are in weak form and semi-strong form, which means that information is efficiently delivered in semi-strong form (Copeland et al., 2014).[2] However, all information delivered is not symmetry between investors and firms: managers who have a better understanding of firms are superior to investors. Information asymmetry can affect decision making in firms including decision making about financing. Although issuance, bankruptcy and agency costs and tax benefits are also considered when making a decision about financing (Myers and Majluf, 1984; Jensen and Meckling, 1976; Kraus and Litzenberger, 1973), this chapter focuses on information asymmetry.

Buyers use general probability distribution expected in a market to judge the quality of purchases (Akerlof, 1970). There is an incentive for sellers to sell products with inferior quality if there is information asymmetry between buyers and sellers. It is eventually possible to lower the average quality of goods and to lead to the decreased size of the market. Akerlof (1970) shows the problem of information asymmetry using the example of automobiles markets and proposes that insurance and credit markets can have the problem of information asymmetry. Especially in credit markets in underdeveloped countries, high interest rates are attributed to high information asymmetry between creditors and debtors. Academic literature related to information asymmetry and financing is classified into two kinds of studies: the relationship between information asymmetry and financing of firms and the reduction of information asymmetry occurred in financial markets.

1. Information asymmetry and corporate financing decision

The most influential theory on the relationship between information asymmetry and corporate financing decision would be the pecking order theory (Myers and Majluf, 1984; Myers, 1984). External investors generally do not know the prospect of firms better than owner-managers, whereas managers have an incentive to offer a positive assessment of their potential but may be reluctant to give negative information. When there is information asymmetry between participants, the pecking order theory gives an explanation that firms might finance capital in the order from retained earnings to external equity financing. It is the order of costs of information asymmetry from the least to the greatest. Firms prefer retained earnings with no information asymmetry as their main source of capital, and the next is debt. The last of the order is external equity financing with big information asymmetry between managers and investors. Therefore, there is no optimal capital structure, and it would just depend on each firm's history under the pecking order theory.

There are many studies to test the pecking order theory. In most studies, information asymmetry has an effect on financing decision and large firms tend to prefer debt to external equity. While research literature of the pecking order theory is to test empirically whether firms were financed according to predictions, some studies are to analyze whether information asymmetry affects financing decision virtually.

Bharath et al. (2009) test whether information asymmetry is an important determinant of capital structure decision. As a result of the analysis, it does affect the capital structure decisions of the US companies. The larger the information asymmetry of firms, the larger the rate of money funded by debt-issuance to cover financing deficits. They infer that 'on average, firms in the highest information asymmetry issue 30 cents of debt more than firms in the lowest decile for every dollar of financing deficit to cover'.

Kim et al. (2012) conduct similar research using the sample of Korean firms. Controlling determinants of the capital structure such as tangible assets, growth opportunities, and firm size, Debt financing increase as information asymmetry increase. The results prove that information asymmetry affects the financial decision of Korean firms. Fazzari and Athey (1987) add a new dimension of information asymmetry to the traditional investment model that investment is determined by the costs of capital. Unless there was information asymmetry in the capital market, funds would be distributed efficiently according to the costs of capital. However, because asymmetric information exists in reality and it leads to a financial constraint on the investment of a firm, the availability of internal cash flow is important to the firm's ability to invest.

As research questions become sophisticated, recent papers have another implication. The pecking order theory may be fitted to small and medium-sized enterprises (hereafter, SMEs) because the smaller the firm size is, the larger the asymmetric information is (Frank and Goyal, 2003). Peterson and Shulman (1987) suggest a model relating the capital structure of small firms to their ages. In the beginning, the debt ratio of firms is low because the first investment comes from founders and banks are reluctant to provide a loan due to information asymmetry. As small firms build a relationship with banks, it is possible to borrow loans from banks. As the problem of asymmetric information is reduced, their debt ratio becomes higher. When they grow beyond a certain size, the debt ratio is lowered by issuing stocks for raising funds. Watson and Wilson (2002) test whether SMEs' capital structure decision is consistent with the pecking order theory using the sample of 626 SMEs in the UK. They show that the group of SMEs with high asymmetric information run by the owner-manager is most suitable to the pecking order theory. When debts are separated into categories, the explanatory power of the model increases and SMEs tend to prefer a specific debt (e.g. hire purchase liabilities) to other debts. Thus, they argue that there is a pecking order within subsets of debts. Beck et al. (2008) find that SMEs do not use more leasing compared to large firms whereas they use more informal financing, especially in developing countries. Bolton and Freixas (2000) make a model of the pecking order theory including not only common shares and bonds but also bank loans. They show that firms have different priorities for raising capital depending on their risks. The riskiest firms such as ventures or start-ups either are unable to raise money or have only an option to issue equity, and safer firms can obtain bank loans that are the cheapest method of flexible financing for them. The safest firms prefer stocks or bonds issuance through the capital market to avoid paying the intermediation cost.

2.   *Information asymmetry and costs of capital*

The other stream of literature related to asymmetric information and financing concerns how asymmetric information affects the costs of capital and which institutions are needed to reduce information asymmetry.

Information asymmetry can have an effect on the costs of capital. Investors demand a higher rate of return to hold stocks with private information than the public (Easley and O'Hara, 2004). While investors with private information are easy to shift their portfolio given new information, uninformed investors are disadvantaged due to the lack of opportunity to adjust their portfolio, thereby taking more risk. Thus, uninformed investors require a higher rate of return. Cho and Jo (2007) use two proxies for information asymmetry: volatility of daily rate of return and prediction errors of analysts. They show the results that the higher the volatility and the bigger the prediction errors, that is the larger the information asymmetry, the higher the costs of equity capital. Ko and Lee (2012) show that there is a positive relationship between information asymmetry and the costs of debt capital. They find that firms with high information asymmetry have a higher cost of debt capital. Additionally, the relationship is stronger when firms are financially distressed. In summary, information asymmetry can decrease the costs of debt capital as well as the costs of equity capital.

An important part of studies on asymmetric information and financing is the research regarding system improvement in order to reduce information asymmetry and the costs of capital in capital markets. Beck et al. (2008) illustrate the importance of the development of financial markets. They find that leasing finance does not play a role of meeting financial needs of small firms in countries with underdeveloped institutions and the use of leasing finance has a positive relationship with the development of financial institutions and capital markets. In addition, property rights protection plays an important role in financing from external sources such as a bank, stock issuance, and lease, particularly more important for SMEs. SMEs benefit from better protection of property rights in terms of accessing sources of capital. This point is similar to Levine (2005), who asserts that the good quality of financial services by the entire financial and legal systems for financial development are important in economic growth of countries regardless of bank-based systems or market-based systems.

Corporate disclosure is critical for efficient capital markets because it is a method to reduce information asymmetry. Healy and Palepu (2001) provide three ways for firms to disclose their information; regulated financial reports including financial statements and notes, voluntary disclosure including investor relations meeting and press releases, and information intermediaries such as financial analysts and rating agencies. Healy and Palepu state that regulated financial reports provide investors with valuable information, analysts play an important role in improving market efficiency and voluntary disclosure and communication lead to the increased liquidity of stocks, the decreased cost of capital. Easley and O'Hara (2004) also propose the selection of accounting standards, corporate disclosure policies, and attracting active analysts as methods of reducing the costs of capital.

IV. Financing consumer cooperatives

1. Information asymmetry caused by the lack of financial markets for cooperatives

There are mainly two types of financial markets: direct financial markets called *capital markets* and indirect markets including banks. Direct financial markets are markets where suppliers and demanders of funds can directly transact business as contracting parties while in indirect financial markets funds are brokered by financial intermediaries connecting suppliers and demanders of funds through deposits and loans. For example, in direct markets demanders of funds issue stocks and bonds in order to raise money and suppliers provide money by buying that stocks and bonds directly. In indirect markets, financial transactions are carried out by financial institutions like banks that play both roles that raise money from depositors and supply money to borrowers. Financial markets perform various roles and one of the roles is to decrease costs and hours to collect information necessary for financial transactions. If financial markets work efficiently, investors could make more reasonable decisions and borrowers could be financed easier because they are evaluated about their risks and so on (Bank of Korea, 2016).

Cooperatives cannot issue stocks and even bonds in Korea, and thus they cannot raise money through capital markets. It means that there is no market to transfer information efficiently to investors, so the extent of information asymmetry between cooperatives and investors would be bigger than that of IOBs. Investors could not have any information to assess the value of projects which cooperatives have, which means bigger uncertainty on behalf of investors. The lack of information transaction due to the lack of capital markets could cause cooperatives to underinvest even if they have profitable projects.

Financial institutions such as banks perform functions connecting suppliers and demanders of funds. Banks hold expert knowledge and skill on borrowers' credit analysis and have continuous and repetitive financial transactions with borrowers. They can obtain information about borrowers, mitigate information asymmetry, and eventually increase the efficiency of supplying money (Bank of Korea, 2011). Consumer cooperatives, however, have only short histories since the related laws enforced respectively in 1999 and 2012. Therefore, it is not enough time for banks to collect and accumulate information about them and there are not enough opportunities to have the financial transaction with them.

Unlisted firms as well as cooperatives can have trouble in using financial markets with the role of transferring information. Unlisted companies do not tap into capital markets easily and are difficult to prepare information systems for communication with external. Thus, many SMEs experience difficulties for growth due to the restriction of financing caused by information asymmetry between SMEs and investors (Becchetti and Trovato, 2002).

SMEs in Korea have tried to solve the restriction problems of financing caused by information asymmetry through collaterals and have been financed mostly from banks and family and friends, not from capital markets (Kim, 2002). A survey shows that external finance of SMEs consists of bank loans 79%, policy loans 15.1%, bonds 3.3%, stock 0.0%, private loans 1.0% in 2015 (Korea Federation of Small and Medium Business, 2015). SMEs depend highly on banks, whereas the ratio of the direct financial markets is very low. In another study, SMEs seem to use more informal funds than large corporations (Beck et al., 2008). Informal investors, so-called 4Fs including founders, family, friends, foolhardy strangers perform an important role in funding for SMEs and ventures. In 2003, informal investors provided funds over 100 billion USD to 3.5 million start-ups and small firms in the United States (Bygrave, 2004). Moreover, about three in every one hundred adults invest in other's business in the sample period (Reynolds et al., 2004). 43.7% of the investors invested in a family member's business, 29.2% in friends or neighbors', 8.9% in relatives, 8.9% in their colleagues', 9.3% in strangers' (Reynolds et al., 2004: 58).

2. Information asymmetry and members' participation in capital

Consumer cooperatives are still unfamiliar to banks and other financial institutions although it has been 17 years since the law was enacted, and cooperatives under the Framework Act on Cooperative experience trouble with financing as well. Major financing methods of cooperatives in Korea are as follows: loans from affiliates 38.9%, government subsidies 20.4%, loans from financial institutions 18.5% (Lee, 2014). The burden to collaterals and guarantees, excessive documents, and the proof of financial performance and value of projects are identified as the difficulties of financing, respectively, at 28.3%, 19.7%, 18.1%, and 11.4%. These problems seem to be primarily concerned with information asymmetry.

Consumer cooperatives may have structurally less asymmetric information between them and their members than between them and external investors. Members establish consumer cooperatives so that they purchase products and/or services which they want. Members are not only the users but also the owners of cooperatives. That is the reason why cooperatives can require members (and owners) to invest the capital needed to run a business. Much of information exchange takes place between members and their cooperatives in the ways of democratic governance and activities within the cooperatives (Choi et al., 2014). Generally, cooperatives try to communicate with their members. For instance, they make efforts to reflect members' opinion in their policies and to transfer their status, vision and management policies to their members. Members have the right to attend a general meeting and to vote on bills. Also, they have chances to participate in community meetings, clubs, educations and activities in cooperatives. Especially in Korea, many consumer cooperatives and their boards of directors emphasize and promote members to participate in their governance, community meetings, clubs, education, and activities (Choi, 2013; Kim et al., 2013). This means that the extent of information asymmetry would be less between cooperatives and their members than between cooperatives and external investors. Thus, it could decrease the costs of capital to borrow money from members instead of banks. Consumer cooperatives have another advantage in funding. They have a lot of members relatively compared to other types of cooperatives. Once consumer cooperatives are able to persuade their members to attend funding, it would be easier and faster to raise capital for business. This is because it is possible to decrease the amount of investment per member due to many members in consumer cooperatives, which means the decrease of risk per member. The probability of success to finance capital for cooperatives would increase as risk per a member decrease.

Andrews (2015) investigates capital instruments that the largest 300 cooperatives and mutuals are using. Many of them are using many instruments including bonds, commercial paper, leasing, loans by members, loans by banks, member shares, participation shares, and so on. However, consumer cooperatives in Korea can use only loans and member shares. Loans are mainly divided into member and bank loans. The extent of information asymmetry with banks would be bigger than that with members for consumer cooperatives. It may be speculated that the difference between the rates of bank loans and those of member loans is the difference between the costs of asymmetric information of banks and those of members. Generally, member shares include basic shares, optional investment shares, and preference shares. In Korea, consumer cooperatives cannot issue preference shares, and the amounts of money through basic shares are too small to raise enough capital. Although optional investment shares are a useful means to raise money for specific business projects, they have uncertainty on dividend pay-out. There is the other uncertainty which is relevant to the investment term, since member shares must be repayable when members withdraw from their cooperatives. The due date for loans is set in the beginning so loans have a clear investment term, but in the case of optional investment shares, the due date is not clear at least in Korea. This would be a kind of asymmetric information between cooperatives and members because cooperatives do not have information about the time when they leave and the shares are repayable. Having these factors consumer cooperatives may have their own pecking order in financing. Firstly, they use retained earnings, which do not have information asymmetry. Next, they might try to finance capital with member loans, and then optional investment shares. Finally, they use external loans, in which information asymmetry is relatively bigger. This study suggests the following proposition:

> Proposition: Consumer cooperatives have their own pecking order in financing: retained earnings, member loans, optional investment shares, and external loans.

Figure 5.1 The pecking order of consumer cooperatives according to information asymmetry

V. The case of iCOOP

iCOOP is a federation that consists of 98 primary consumer cooperatives as of 2018. It has the largest sales and the second largest number of members. Its business focuses on eco-friendly food and products based on ethical production and consumption. Most members decide to join iCOOP primary consumer cooperatives (hereafter iCOOP PCCs) to purchase safe and trustworthy food and products (iCOOP Cooperative Institute, 2013). In the beginning, only online business started in the process of integrating logistic and improving management since 2000, and store business started in 2006 with its own brand 'Natural Dream'. In addition to the business, iCOOP and its members propose and practice social agendas from the safety of food and the movement for consumer rights to extended themes such as fair trade, ethical consumption practice movement, and how farmers and consumers are satisfied together in the distribution process.

The first event that iCOOP borrowed money from members was the fire of a logistics center. In order to raise funds for recovery, the directors of the boards decided to borrow money from members, executives, and employees (Yeom, 2018). After that, iCOOP has utilized member loans actively and the loans turn out to be an important means in developing iCOOP rapidly. As iCOOP PCCs opened their offline stores since 2006, member loans have been more actively utilized even in the level of primary cooperatives until now. This study will look at the member loans of iCOOP PCCs in the perspective of information asymmetry.

There is evidence to support the argument that iCOOP could use member loans due to less information asymmetry. First, it was possible to borrow capital from members without tangible assets. Seo and Choi (2016) show the positive relationship between leverage ratio and tangible asset ratio in iCOOP PCCs. It is generally suggested that the positive relationship between leverage ratio and tangible asset ratio follows the static trade-off theory, not the pecking order theory. Under the trade-off theory, tangible assets could increase debts because tangible assets could decrease bankruptcy costs and be used as collaterals. However, they interpret the result differently because the cooperatives were able to finance capital without tangible assets as collateral. Table 5.1 provides the relationship among leverage ratio, tangible asset ratio and the period of operating stores in iCOOP PCCs. The leverage ratio and the tangible asset ratio are the largest in the first year after opening new stores in type 1. After the first year, both of them decrease monotonically. In type 2, the first year after opening new stores shows the highest values in the change of the leverage ratio and change of the tangible asset ratio and the subsequent years show the negative values. These results show the cooperatives borrow money first and then buy tangible assets to open stores and repay the loans with earnings from the business. They assert that these results are in accordance with the pecking order theory based on information asymmetry. When they started to run the business, less information asymmetry between the cooperatives and their members enabled to finance the necessary capital in the form of member loans without tangible assets and retained earnings.

Table 5.1 Relationship among leverage ratio, tangible asset ratio, and period of operating stores

		First year	Second year	Third year	Fourth year
Type 1	Number of financial statements	48	47	22	8
	Leverage ratio	52.81	51.63	43.67	26.19
	Tangible assets ratio	33.41	28.37	24.22	13.22
Type 2	Number of financial statements	26	32	20	8
	Change of leverage ratio	18.73	-0.90	-6.87	-15.43
	Change of tangible assets ratio	10.81	-5.57	-3.90	-7.52

Second, the purpose of borrowing money is obvious and easy for members to understand it. The first member loan was to rebuild the damaged logistic center. The subsequent member loans have been for mainly a sort of project businesses – for example, building its own industrial complexes, opening offline stores, purchasing crops in advance, and so on, even though iCOOP raised occasionally member loans for working capital. It was an opportunity for iCOOP PCCs to start new stores in that much more members as well as activists began to participate in member loans. Members decided to run their stores to improve their convenience. The business model is simple. Members set up their stores which are run as a franchise business of iCOOP and they use the stores. To do that, a lot of money[3] was needed, and the decision was made to raise money from members. Although it was possible to be financed with member loans which have less information asymmetry than others, it took a long time to raise enough money in the first time in almost primary cooperatives. It may have taken a long time for their members to be convinced of the business model. However, when opening subsequent stores, iCOOP PCCs were able to raise enough capital much faster. It was possible because of the understanding and trust of members about the business model at that time. While they are running the first store, their members understood and had confidence in the store business, which reduces the information asymmetry between the cooperatives and their members.

'As the first store became stabilized with members' usage and participation, we were able to start the second and the third stores. In the second and the third stores, many members have lent their money without explaining much since they understand the store business'.[4]

The ties between iCOOP PCCs and their members are stronger as they build trust. For example, B iCOOP PCC has operated the first store successfully so as to make a decision to open the second store. This time, it took just three days to raise the capital, about 467,000 USD, in optional investment shares and member loans.[5] It was a big difference from the case of the first store three years ago. At that time, it took six months to collect the same amount of money.[6]

Third, cooperatives have structurally the advantage of communication and iCOOP PCCs have utilized the advantage, which also lowers asymmetric information. According to Birchall (2012), cooperatives seek to align the interests of members with directors of boards and managers, which is related to business success in terms of member control. In other words, members have their voice and chances to participate in the governance of their cooperatives. In this process, their opinion can be delivered to management, and it is possible that their interests are aligned with the cooperatives. For example, the UK Cooperative Bank revised its mission and strategy through the market surveys of member attitudes and opinions in the 1990s and has become a leader in ethical banks (Davis, 1999). It is thought that it is possible to be vice versa. It is structurally easy for cooperatives to communicate with their members and to transfer information about their situation and strategy. It would decrease the gap of information asymmetry between them, which helps cooperatives to raise money from their members.

Choi (2013) shows that the effort of boards of directors to identify and incorporate needs of their members into cooperatives' policies affect positively not only the participation of members in community meetings and education programs at a 1% significant level but also the economic participation measured by the number of member loans, at a 10% significant level. In the case of iCOOP, a board of directors is supposed to communicate with its members in the decision-making process (e.g. a general meeting of members, committees and so on), and tries to reflect their voices in practice through town meetings and social clubs. There 945 town meetings, 912 social club, and 10,103 participants in whole primary cooperatives as of 2017 (iCOOP Korea, 2017). These systems play a meaningful role to exchange information about the needs and wants of members and the mission, vision, and direction of the cooperatives.

Education programs are also a good way to reduce information asymmetry. iCOOP federation and its primary cooperatives offer a variety of education programs for their members from beginners to directors. In 2017, total of 85,009 members participated in education programs officially. These programs have turned lay members into activists, which is important in creating the democratic governance of cooperatives (Kim, 2018). iCOOP states that their education is not a one-way transfer of knowledge, but practice process where activities and reflection continue to repeat. We can find out in the materials of the general meeting of primary cooperatives that they have communicated with their members through town meetings as well as general meetings and have held several business presentations for their members in order to explain the purpose and meaning of store business and persuade the economic participation of the members before starting store business.

VI. Discussion

Many prior studies about financing cooperatives have focused on the property rights theory, including residual claims and residual rights of control. However, it seems that they can explain partially the trouble of financing capital in cooperatives. Rather, it is thought that cooperatives experience the difficulty in raising money because there is no place where information exchange between cooperatives and investors happens. Therefore, this study suggests the proposition that consumer cooperatives have their own pecking order in financing: retained earnings, member loans, optional investment shares, and banks and external loans.

Under the situation of little retained earnings, iCOOP has used mainly member loans which have less information asymmetry than others. This study proposes three clues showing that the reason why iCOOP was able to use member loans is that of less information asymmetry. First, iCOOP and its primary cooperatives were able to borrow capital from members without tangible assets. Second, the purpose of borrowing capital is obvious and easy for members to understand it. Third, cooperatives have structurally the advantage of communication and iCOOP PCCs try to utilize the advantage, which decreases asymmetric information. They are still using member loans today while rarely using bank loans or external capital.

What policies and systems should we prepare in order to satisfy the needs of capital in cooperatives? First, the current financial market systems and related laws should be improved to adapt to the characteristic of cooperatives. It is likely that the current systems and ideas such as capital markets, investor protection systems and property rights focusing on IOBs, are not proper for cooperatives. Inappropriate systems can prevent organizations and firms from growing. Even if small firms usually use fewer bank loans, it is likely that small firms in countries developing the protection of property rights use more bank loans (Beck et al., 2008). In other words, the development of the systems helps small firms to more easily access formal capital methods like bank loans. If laws and systems for cooperatives are developed, they would flourish. In particular, it is important that member loans should be admitted legally as a means of financing in Korea. Many countries already recognize member loans legally. In the United States, the Supreme Court decision about a type of member loans was important guidance for consumer cooperatives in 1990 and provided opportunities to utilize member loans (Lushin, 1991).

Second, means to reduce information asymmetry with investors should be developed so that financial markets for cooperatives can emerge and function efficiently. Healy and Palepu (2001) review regulated financial reports, voluntary communication and information intermediaries in methods of corporate disclosure. They argue that demand for disclosure results from information asymmetry. This chapter concentrates on financial reporting still incomplete in Korea. Financial reporting (regulated financial reports) can provide investors with valuable information. Cooperatives should provide members and internal and external stakeholders with clear financial information. With it, members and potential members are likely to be interested and participate in their cooperatives, and investors and external stakeholders can evaluate the financial performance of cooperatives more exactly. Thus, the costs of capital would be able to decrease. However, there is no criteria of financial reports for cooperatives, no system of financial reporting, and no place of disclosing and obtaining the financial information of cooperatives in Korea. These systems are required to reduce information asymmetry and to facilitate financing for cooperatives.

Notes

1 The Ministry of Economy and Finance is in charge of the Framework Act on Cooperatives in Korea.
2 Fama (1970)

- Weak-form efficiency: No investor can make excess returns by developing trading rules based on historical price or return information
- Semistrong-form efficiency: No investor can make excess returns from trading rules based on any publicly available information.
- Strong-form efficiency: No investor can make excess returns using any information, whether publicly available or not

3 It varies depending on stores but needs roughly 500–800 million KRW (approximately 467,000–747,000 USD).
4 Jo, a chairperson of an iCOOP primary consumer cooperative (Kim et al., 2012: 58).
5 Each ratio of optional investment shares and member loans to total sum is approximately 20% and 80%.
6 Kim (2013).

References

Akerlof, G. A. (1970) 'The Market for 'Lemons': Quality Uncertainty and the Market Mechanism.' *Quarterly Journal of Economics*, 84: 488–500.

Andrews, A. M. (2015) *Survey of Cooperative Capital*. Madison, WI: Filene Research Institute.

Bank of Korea (2011) *Urinaraui geumyungjedo* [Financial System in South Korea]. Seoul, Korea: Bank of Korea.

Bank of Korea (2016) *Urinaraui geumyungsijang* [Financial Market in South Korea]. Seoul, Korea: Bank of Korea.

Becchetti, L., and Trovato, G. (2002) 'The Determinants of Growth for Small and Medium Sized Firms: The Role of the Availability of External Finance.' *Small Business Economics*, 19: 291–306.

Beck, T., Demirgüç-Kunt, A., and Maksimovic, V. (2008) 'Financing Patterns Around the World: Are Small Firms Different?' *Journal of Financial Economics*, 89: 467–487.

Bharath, S. T., Pasquariello, P., and Wu, G. (2009) 'Does Asymmetric Information Drive Capital Structure Decisions?' *Review of Financial Studies*, 22: 3211–3243.

Birchall, J. (2012) 'The Comparative Advantages of Member-Owned Businesses.' *Review of Social Economy*, 70(3): 263–294.

Bolton, P., and Freixas, X. (2000) 'Equity, Bonds, and Bank Debt: Capital Structure and Financial Market Equilibrium Under Asymmetric Information.' *Journal of Political Economy*, 108: 324–351.

Bygrave, W. D. (2004) *Founders, Family, Friends, and Fools*. New York, NY: Bloomberg.

Chaddad, F. R., and Cook, M. L. (2004) 'Understanding New Cooperative Models: An Ownership-Control Rights Typology.' *Applied Economic Perspectives and Policy*, 26: 348–360.

Cho, J. S., and Jo, M. H. (2007) 'Jeongbobidaechingi jagijabonbiyonge michineun yeonghyang' [The Relation Between Information Asymmetry and the Cost of Capital]. *Korean Academic Society of Accounting*, 12: 269–288.

Choi, E. J. (2013) *Sobijasaenghwalhyeopdongjohap jibaegujoga gyeongyeongseonggwae michineun yeonghyang* [The Effect of Corporate Governance on Performance of Consumer Cooperatives in Korea]. Master Dissertation, Sungkonghoe University, Seoul, Korea.

Choi, E. J., Choi, W., Jang, S., and Park, S. (2014) 'Does the Effectiveness of Board of Directors Affect Firm Performance of Consumer Cooperatives? The Case of iCOOP KOREA.' *Annals of Public and Cooperative Economics*, 85: 371–386.

Choi, W., and Seo, J.-S. (2014) 'Buchaeui sayongi sobijasaenghwalhyeopdongjohabui jaemuseonggwae michineun yeonghyang' [The Effect of Leverage on Financial Performance in Consumer Cooperatives: The Case of iCOOP Korea]. *Social Enterprise Studies*, 7(1): 91–115.

Cook, M. L., and Iliopoulos, C. (1999) 'Beginning to Inform the Theory of the Cooperative Firm: Emergence of the New Generation Cooperative.' *Finnish Journal of Business Economics*, 3: 525–535.

Copeland, T. E., Weston, J. F., and Shastri, K. (2014) *Financial Theory and Corporate Policy: Pearson New International Edition*. Essex, UK: Pearson.

Davis, P. (1999) *Managing the Cooperative Difference: A Survey of the Application of Modern Management Practices in the Cooperative Context*. Geneva: International Labor Organization.

Easley, D., and O'Hara, M. (2004) 'Information and the Cost of Capital.' *Journal of Finance*, 59: 1553–1583.

Fama, E. F. (1970) 'Efficient Capital Markets: A Review of Theory and Empirical Work.' *Journal of Finance*, 25(2): 383–417.

Fama, E. F., and Jensen, M. C. (1983) 'Separation of Ownership and Control.' *Journal of Law and Economics*, 26: 301–325.

Fazzari, S. M., and Athey, M. J. (1987) 'Asymmetric Information, Financing Constraints, and Investment.' *The Review of Economics and Statistics*, 69: 481–487.

Frank, M. Z., and Goyal, V. K. (2003) 'Testing the Pecking Order Theory of Capital Structure.' *Journal of Financial Economics*, 67: 217–248.

Grossman, S. J., and Hart, O. D. (1986) 'The Costs and Benefits of Ownership: A Theory of Vertical and Lateral Integration.' *Journal of Political Economy*, 94: 691–719.

Hansmann, H. (1996) *The Ownership of Enterprise*. Cambridge, MA: Harvard University Press.

Healy, P. M., and Palepu, K. G. (2001) 'Information Asymmetry, Corporate Disclosure, and the Capital Markets: A Review of the Empirical Disclosure Literature.' *Journal of Accounting and Economics*, 31: 405–440.

iCOOP Cooperative Institute (2013) *2012 iCOOP saenghyeop johabwonui sobisaenghwalgwa uisige gwanhan josa* [2012 A Survey on Consumption and Awareness of Members of iCOOP Consumer Cooperative]. Seoul, Korea: iCOOP Cooperative Institute.

iCOOP Korea. (2017) *iCOOP Net's Annual Report*. Gunpo, Korea: iCOOP Union.

International Co-operative Alliance (2013) *Blueprint for a Cooperative Decade*. Brussels: International Cooperative Alliance.

International Co-operative Alliance (eds.) (2016) *The Capital Conundrum for Cooperatives*. Brussels: International Cooperative Alliance.

Jensen, M. C., and Meckling, W. H. (1976) 'Theory of the Firm: Managerial Behavior, Agency Costs and Ownership Structure.' *Journal of Financial Economics*, 3: 305–360.

Kim, A. Y. (2018) 'iCOOP saenghyeobui geobeoneonseu silcheon: 2008–2017, Jiyeokjohabeul jungsimeuro' [Governance Practice of iCOOP Consumer Cooperative: From 2008 to 2017, Focusing on Primary Cooperatives]. In iCOOP Cooperative Institute (eds.), *The Value and Practice of Cooperative People: Twenty Years Old iCOOP*. Seoul, Korea: iCOOP Cooperative Institute, pp. 134–170.

Kim, A. Y., Choi, E. J., and Choi, W. (2013) 'Hanguk sobijasaenghwalhyeopdong-johap isahoeui teukseonge gwanhan siljeungyeongu: iCOOP sobijahwaldongyeon-hapoe saryereul jungsimeuro' [An Empirical Study on Characteristics of Board of Directors in Consumer Cooperatives: The Case of iCOOP Korea]. *Korean Journal of Cooperative Studies*, 31(1): 27–55.

Kim, A. Y., Ki, N. C., Kim, D. H., Min, A., and Jo, H. S. (2012) 'Jwadamhoe: Hanguk saenghyeobui jabon jodal hyeonsil' [Round-Table: Some Cooperators in the Field Talk About Real Difficulties of Financing]. *Cooperatives Journal*, 9(Winter), Seoul, Korea: iCOOP Cooperative Institute.

Kim, D. W., Jung, M. G., and Kim, B. G. (2012) 'Jeongbobidaechingeun jabonjujo uisagyeoljeonge yeonghyangeul michineunga?' [Does Asymmetric Information Affect Capital Structure Decision?]. *Korean Journal of Business Administration*, 25: 767–787.

Kim, E. N. (2013) 'Juindoen sobijadeul daehyeongmateuwa matjjang tteuda' [Consumer-Owners Fight Against Mega-Mart]. *SisaIn News Magazine*. www.sisain.co.kr/?mod=news&act=articleView&idxno=15360 (accessed 17 January 2013).

Kim, M. K. (2002) 'Bisangjang, bideungnok jungsogieobui jaemurebeoriji gyeoljeonge gwanhan yeongu' [A Study on the Determinants of Leverage in Unlisted Small and Medium Enterprises]. *Korean Journal of Financial Management*, 19: 33–66.

Ko, Y. W., and Lee, S. C. (2012) 'jeongbobidaechinggwa tainjabonbiyongui gwangye yeongu' [Information Asymmetry and Cost of Debt Capital]. *Korean International Accounting Review*, 43: 41–64.

Korea Federation of Small and Medium Business (2015) *2015nyeondo jungsogieop geumyungiyong mit aerosiltae* [The Utilization of Finance and Difficulty of Small and Medium Sized Firms in 2015]. Seoul, Korea: Korea Federation of Small and Medium Business.

Kraus, A., and Litzenberger, R. H. (1973) 'A State-Preference Model of Optimal Financial Leverage.' *Journal of Finance*, 28: 911–922.

Lee, B. Y. (2014) *2014 nyeon seoulsojae sahoejeok gyeongjegieop jageumjodal josabogoseo* [The Survey of Financing of Social Economy Organization in Seoul, 2014]. Seoul, Korea: Korea Social Investment.

Levine, R. (2005) 'Finance and Growth: Theory and Evidence.' In Philippe, A., and Steven, D. (eds.), *Handbook of Economic Growth*. Amsterdam: North Holland Publishing Company, pp. 865–934.

Lim, Y. S. (2004) 'Hyeopdongjohabui saeroun jabonjodal' [New Financing of Cooperatives]. In *Monthly Investigation of Agricultural Cooperative*, 559. Seoul, Korea: National Agricultural Cooperative Federation, pp. 1–16.

Lund, M. (2013) *Cooperative Equity and Ownership: An Introduction*. Madison, WI: University of Wisconsin Center for Cooperatives.

Lushin, L. (1991) *Securities Laws and Co-op Member Loan Programs*. Cooperative Grocer Network. www.grocer.coop/articles/securities-laws-and-co-op-member-loan-programs.

Mazzarol, T. (2009) *Cooperative Enterprise: A Discussion Paper & Literature Review.* Crawley, WA: University of Western Australia.

Milgrom, P. R., and Roberts, J. D. (1992) *Economics, Organization and Management.* Upper Saddle River, NJ: Prentice Hall.

Myers, S. C. (1984) 'The Capital Structure Puzzle.' *Journal of Finance*, 39(3): 574–592.

Myers, S. C., and Majluf, N. S. (1984) 'Corporate Financing and Investment Decisions When Firms Have Information that Investors Do Not Have.' *Journal of Financial Economics*, 13: 187–221.

Peterson, R., and Shulman, J. (1987) 'Capital Structure of Growing Small Firms: A 12-Country Study on Becoming Bankable.' *International Small Business Journal*, 5: 10–22.

Reynolds, P. D., Bygrave, W. D., Autio, E., and Babson College. (2004) *GEM 2003 Global Report.* Wellesley, MA: Babson College.

Seo, J.-S., and Choi, W. (2016) 'What Determinants Affect the Capital Structure of Consumer Co-operatives? The Case of iCOOP Korea.' *Annals of Public and Cooperative Economics*, 87(1): 117–135.

Shim, I. S. (2015) 'Hyeopdongjohapgibonbeopsang ilbanhyeopdongjohabui jageumjodal beomnie gwanhan yeongu' [Legal Analysis on the Funding Resources of General Cooperatives Under the Framework Act on Cooperatives of Korea]. *Advanced Commercial Law Review*, 72: 1–55.

Watson, R., and Wilson, N. (2002) 'Small and Medium Size Enterprise Financing: A Note on Some of the Empirical Implications of a Pecking Order.' *Journal of Business Finance & Accounting*, 29: 557–578.

Yeom, C. H. (2018) 'iCOOP saenghyeobui jeongchak sigi: 1197nyeonbuteo 2007nyeonkkaji' [The Settlement Period of iCOOP: From 1997 to 2007]. In iCOOP Cooperative Institute (eds.), *The Value and Practice of Cooperative People, Twenty Years Old iCOOP*. Seoul, Korea: iCOOP Cooperative Institute, pp. 11–23.

6 Consumer cooperative brand identity

Sukhee Youn and Sanghoon Lee

I. Introduction

Brand identity is the overall message of how the company aspires to be perceived by its target customers and society, which plays an important role in corporate marketing, distinguishing its products and services from rival brands and influencing on the consumer's decision. The clearer the brand identity is, the more easily consumers recognize the brand, which becomes a competitive advantage for a company to persuade consumers (Aaker, 1996; Kapferer, 2012; Keller and Lehmann, 2006).

However, the brand is abstract and symbolic, and the outcome of time and efforts for the brand to be perceived by consumers is uncertain. It hinders a company from actively investing and establishing a strategy for brand management (De Chernatony et al., 2000; Aaker, 1996; Kapferer, 2012). It is more difficult for cooperatives led by a board of non-professionals to focus on marketing and brand management (Hardesty, 2005; Beverland, 2007). Cooperatives based on the principle of user benefit experience lack of capital to invest in brand promotion and advertisement due to low price margins and are likely to have the 'horizon problem' that makes the cooperatives' members reluctant to invest in product development and marketing in the long term (Jensen and Meckling, 1979; Hardesty, 2005; Novkovic, 2008).

Indeed, most cooperatives in Korea seemed to have difficulty in building a brand and marketing (Lee et al., 2015). However, cooperatives also need a stable return to keep their businesses running, which requires developing and managing brands that increase awareness of their business and foster positive images and trust (Aaker, 1996; Beverland, 2007). Cooperatives must differentiate themselves in niche markets or have a price premium for their private brand in order to survive in this competitive retail market (Hardesty, 2005). It is possible for them to create their own distinctiveness, providing excellent services or securing their own distribution channel. Consumer cooperatives brand can deliver the principles and social values of co-ops as human associations, and at the same time guarantee the product quality and trust of producer and supplier as a retailer (Aaker, 1996; Lee, 2013; Beverland, 2007).

Korea's four major consumer cooperatives – namely, iCOOP, Hansalim, Dure, Happycoop – have grown rapidly since their establishment of the 1980s, clearly showing their brand identity as an 'ecological production and product distributor' that meets consumers' needs to have safe food and environment.

Those four consumer cooperatives were established to solve food safety and environmental problems through eco-friendly product retail business and ultimately aimed to create a better world for both consumers and producers. They were similar in that all of them sought to 'live happily all together' and do business directly with eco-friendly producers, but they were different in their founding philosophy, movement direction and leading members at that time.

Each leading member from the farmer's rural movement, religious social movement, the labor movement and women's movement established their own cooperatives with different visions (Jeong, 2006). The cooperative movement was more than just the exchange value of goods buying eco-friendly products (Shin, 2011; Chang and Lee, 2009). iCOOP promoted 'ethical consumerism', Hansalim proposed 'the idea of life' that claimed, 'all living things are precious' and 'a grain of rice has a universe in it,' Dure presented 'co-operation among our daily lives', and Happycoop (then Minwoohoe cooperative) suggested 'women's rights and happiness'.

Despite its own distinctive vision and different historical background, their images became indistinctive since their businesses have centered on eco-friendly products and their forces of the social movement have weakened. They have faced fierce competition among eco-friendly retailers as the organic market has expanded, and their own brand identity of consumer cooperatives as eco-friendly retailers has weakened as well. Also, their own value and momentum as human associations have been deteriorated since the number of members increased rapidly and the generation of members has changed. Therefore, it is timely to identify the brand identity of each cooperative and differentiation of brand identity, which could provide implications for strategic positioning in brand management. Research questions for this study are as follows:

> Research Question 1: What are the brand identities in consumer cooperatives pursuing?
>
> Research Question 2: What are the similarities and differences between the brand identity of consumer cooperatives?

II.   Theoretical review

1.   *Brand identity*

Brand identity can be defined as an overall message of the images that a company wants to be perceived by the target customer and society, which is a matter of how a company identifies itself (de Chernatony and Cottam, 2006; Harris and de Chernatony, 2001; Kapferer, 2012). The clearer the brand identity, the easier it is for customers to distinguish and recognize (Harris and de Chernatony, 2001; Kapferer, 2012). Strong brand identity increases the potential purchasing power, affects customer loyalty and plays an important role in marketing communication and promotion, which results in the company's sustainable competitive advantage (Harris and Goode, 2004; He et al., 2012; Upshaw, 1995). Building a brand identity must be the first step in marketing strategy because it suggests the company's future direction that implies the company's vision, mission and core values, and it is effective to differentiate and deliver its brand (Kapferer, 2012).

2. *Elements of brand identity*

Ethos, goals and values of an organization could create its brand identity and presented a model of brand management (Harris and de Chernatony, 2001). Brand identity consists of six elements, such as vision, culture, positioning, personality, relationship and reputation. The brand management model (de Chernatony, 1999) shows the process of building a brand identity as revolving around the identification and narrowing the gaps between a brand's identity and its reputation.

Kapferer (2012) and Aaker (1996) included tangible aspects like a physical characteristic, the scope and quality of a product into the elements of brand identity, while Harris and de Chernatony (2001) emphasized on intangible elements of brand identity. Kapferer (2012) insisted that brand identity should be broken down into six components, such as physique, culture, personality, relationship, self-image and reflection, and also that consistent messages and products of brand identity should be provided in order to build a strong brand. Aaker (1996) suggested four perspectives – brand as a product, an organization, a personality, and a symbol converged together to form a core identity. The brand as a product reminds of product attributes, quality, uses; the brand as an organization is considered of characteristics of the organization; the brand as a person regarded that brand itself can have personality like a human being; the brand as symbol means a metaphor, visual imagery, heritage and a connection to a specific brand and favorable impression for a product.

Scholars have different views on what brand identity is and how it is consisted of, but largely they could be divided into two categories: tangible and intangible elements. The former can be seen, felt or noticed, such as brand logos, packaging, product attributes, characteristics and slogan. The latter is abstract and hard to measure, like vision, mission, culture, core values and positioning. They interact with each other and then create consistent messages that can build a strong brand identity (Seo, 2014; Kapferer, 2012). The elements of brand identity from theory review can be explained as follows.

1) *Vision*

Vision provides the value that shapes, directs and guides the purpose of brand existence (Collins and Porras, 1996). Vision is a preferred future for the brand, 'what do we hope to become?', and includes the essence and core values that do not change easily (Kapferer, 2012). Most companies and organizations state their vision on the webpage or vision statement which provides stakeholders with a picture of what their ideal brand is (Aaker, 1992; Aaker, 1996; Gurley et al., 2015).

2)   *Mission*

The mission is one of the reasons why an organization exists and the purpose of establishment, which distinguishes it from other organizations (Urde, 2003). Establishing a mission shapes, directs and guides how to manage an organization or business, which will be the foundations of its members' responsibility and pride. While mission focuses on the present and describes the objectives of the organization in the short term, vision aims for the future and depicts its aspiration in the long term (Collins and Porras, 1996; Gurley et al., 2015).

3)   *Culture*

Culture is a unique style of survival such as the shared values, beliefs, and behavioral norms that have been formed over many years by the CEOs and all the members of a company (Schein, 2010; Urde, 2003). Culture, like vision, serves as a guide to set a direction of a brand and an organization and as a guideline for its members (Harris and de Chernatony, 2001; Schein, 2010). A brand represents a company's ethos as a visible expression of its culture and plays a key role in brand differentiation (Kapferer, 2012).

4)   *Core values*

Core values are the shared beliefs and behavioral norms of a company that do not change even when time passes and members changes. Core values answer the question, 'how must we behave in order to make our shared vision a reality?' and provide a small set of guiding principles beyond time (Collins and Porras, 1996). Core values connect vision, mission and culture of a company and guide a direction for the way to develop products and service and how to manage its business (Urde, 2003)

5)   *Positioning*

Brand's positioning presents what the brand is, who it is for and what it offers (Harris and de Chernatony, 2001), and that delivers distinctive characteristics and benefits of the brand (Nandan, 2005). It is brand positioning that differentiates a brand from competing brands, emphasizes its distinctiveness, and appeals to customers (Kapferer, 2012).

6)   *Brand name*

A brand name is a symbol representing the characteristics, uses and preferences of products or services as a way of primary communication between producers and consumers, sellers and buyers. Brand name assigns meaning and symbol to real products, services or organizations, which revive its purpose. It shows the benefits of a brand like belief, stability, consistency and status regarding brand identity (Wheeler, 2003).

7) Slogan

A slogan is a concise, powerful phrase or sentence that uses the characteristics, arguments, ideas of product repeatedly over a long period of time to stimulate customers' purchasing behavior as persuasive or descriptive information about the brand (Keller, 2001). Aaker (1996) describes a brand slogan as a way of communicating core values that a company aspires to deliver and compares the slogan to 'ribbons' for 'packaging' because it adds a special sensation.

In order to identify brand identity each consumer cooperatives suggests, the elements of brand identity were recategorized into mission, core values, brand meaning, brand characteristics and vision: mission is the purpose of establishment, core values are the intrinsic principles, brand meaning is what brand name means and aims for, brand characteristics includes attributes and benefits of products and positioning. Other components like culture, personality and relationship were excluded due to the limit of time and methods, in that they are formed over a long period of time interacting within and outside of cooperatives.

3. The brand of Korea's four major consumer cooperatives

1) Natural dream: iCOOP

iCOOP business association was founded in 1997, rooted in local cooperatives led by student movement and the labor movement. It operates 217 retail stores as of 2016 and home delivery service nationwide under the brand name Natural Dream (iCOOP website; iCOOP, 2017). The start was very small and insignificant, as the six local cooperatives in business and financial difficulties united as one to prevent the collapse and to solve managerial issues. The slogan of 'organic food for ordinary people and supply of safe food' was the main idea of the business, and an eco-friendly products distribution system favorable to both producers and consumers were established (iCOOP website). iCOOP integrated a business and logistic system to increase management efficiency, implemented the policy of separating business and movement (iCOOP business association focusing on business, local cooperatives on organizing members and activities). Likewise, brand name and organization name were used differently like Natural Dream and iCOOP. iCOOP declared that 'Natural Dream' meant ethical consumption and ethical production, considering food safety, human rights and global environment (Shin, 2011).

2) Hansalim

Hansalim means 'all living things live together as they were under one roof, and save one another', which is based on its 'philosophy of life' (Hansalim

Moim, 1989). Hansalim was launched in 1986 when farmers activists with the idea of 'life movement' opened a small rice shop called 'Hansalim Farm' in Seoul. It was a part of a farmers' movement in order to get paid the 'right price for right agricultural products'. The purpose and orientation of Hansalim were embodied in the 'Hansalim declaration' announced in 1989 and developed into 'life movement' to practice the lifestyle according to the values and principles of 'revive table food, revive agriculture, revive living things.' The Hansalim movement brought the value of 'life movement' and linked to the business of direct trade between urban consumers and rural farmers, unlike previous consumer cooperatives focused just on a joint purchase. The Hansalim slogan of 'rural farmers for consumers' life, urban consumers for farmers life' spread and influenced all other cooperatives (Kim et al., 2012; Hansalim website; Seo, 2014).

3) Dure cooperatives

It was the beginning of Dure when the seven local cooperatives (Barun Dure, Kyonggi Dure, Anyang YMCA, Buchoen YMCA, Kwangmyeong YMCA, Jumin, Hanwooli) in a metropolitan area joined together to form 'Metropolitan Business Association Ltd.', emphasizing the economy and efficiency of the business (Kim et al., 2012; Kwon, 2012). First, it concentrated its capacity on business systemization to increase efficiency, to which it strengthened CMS (Cash Management Service) automatic transfer to increase cash flow, computerized logistics system, set up an online shopping mall and set up a forecast system to counter instability of demand and supply. Besides, Dure developed a computerization program recording production history and introduced a self-inspection system in order to establish trust between producers and consumers (Dure Consumer Cooperatives' Union, 2017). Dure dreamed of a trustworthy society that values local communities breathing together beyond the sharing of food. Furthermore, it had the vision to create a new world associated with third-world producers through 'fair trade' (Dure website).

4) Happycoop

Since the democratization movement in 1987, a cooperative that was led by the YMCA, religious group and civic groups was organized. Among them, 'Women's Link' was established to organize women's power and encompass women's and housewives' lives as a part of a women's movement (Kim et al., 2012). Women's Link, with a clear identity as a women's movement, has continued to address environmental issues, food safety, women's rights, education and consumerism and so on from the feminist point of view. However, 'Women's Link' within a special framework of a 'women's organization' became diverse and complicated, and there raised a demand for a paradigm shift. So Happycoop separated itself from Women's Link to respond more comprehensibly to community issues involving women (Kim, 2012). The brand name 'Happycoop' was used for local retail stores and home delivery service since 2012. They uphold a vision that promises to spread happiness to their community and others, and aim to create safe food, an alternative economy and a welfare system with women and local communities (Happycoop website).

III. Research methods

1. Data collection

The data collection and analyzing procedure is based on narrative analysis that is appropriate for finding main elements from the abstract concept of brand identity using data collected from the field. A brand is not just 'things' that cannot be measured but 'balance' of complementary features that meet consumers' reason, emotion and their social and cultural needs (Cooper, 1999). To fully understand this complexity, an in-depth approach is necessary to investigate the memory of respondents by applying questions individually (Zaltman, 1997; Grace and O'Cass, 2005). Therefore, this study would describe the narratives of brand identity directly by using a qualitative approach like in-depth interviews and literature reviews (Hastings and Perry, 2000).

The interviewees were selected from the top executives or board members who could present the purpose and vision of cooperative business and movement. The in-depth interviews were conducted based on semi-structured, open-ended questionnaires according to the literature review of brand identity. They were recorded with the consent of research participants and then transcribed with memos. The general characteristics of the interview participants are shown in Table 6.1.

Table 6.1 Interview participants

Brand		Position	Period of working	Gender
Natural Dream	A	Chief executive	17 years	Male
	B	Board member	15 years	Female
	C	Former chief executive	20 years	Male
	D	Board member	19 years	Female
Hansalim	E	Board member	23 years	Female
	F	Chief executive	29 years	Male
	G	Working member	14 years	Female
	H	Chief executive	28 years	Female
Dure	I	Chief executive	24 years	Male
	J	Board member	20 years	Female
	K	Chief executive	20 years	Male
	L	Chief executive	19 years	Male
Happycoop	M	Board member	10 years	Female
	N	Chief manager	8 years	Male
	O	Former board member	17 years	Female
	P	Chief manager	7 years	Female

In addition to the in-depth interviews, secondary data such as annual report, general assembly report, related thesis and websites were referenced. Consumer cooperatives held a general assembly every year that informed its members of current status and future plan of business and activities. The contents of the general assembly report included establishment declaration, history, business strategy and direction, so it could show its mission and vision as core components of brand identity. The websites of all four consumer cooperatives introduce their businesses, corporate images and brand images each cooperative pursues.

2. *Methods of analysis*

The narrative approach used in this study does not have a single 'right way' but have various forms. 'Narrative' can be a phenomenon being studied or a way of analyzing a narrative story that was told (Creswell, 2007). 'Narratives' about the brand identity each cooperative suggests is the subject of research and the method of analysis at the same time in this study. Narrative analysis is the stage where writing based on the texts collected from fields is done and creating meanings of experiences has proceeded. Appropriate paragraphs may be used as a unit of analysis, main themes or ideas that are extracted from the reactions of participants as a method of analysis (Kim, 2013; Creswell, 2007).

The brand identity this study tries to identify is a dynamic concept that presents from the purpose of the organization (mission) to future direction (vision) and also that narratives business managers and working members told. A narrative analysis that is a flexible and open approach would be appropriate because it could capture the complexity, ambiguity and uncertainty of organizations and express them realistically. As Brown (2006) argued, no other approach than narrative analysis can capture them.

The analytical procedure is to classify and categorize common themes and patterns in the process of repeatedly reading and writing data gathered from in-depth interviews and documents. In other words, all the texts from transcriptions of interviews, memos and documents were reviewed and then aligned into significant individual phrases; finally, repetitive and meaningful narratives were found and reconstructed (Chreim, 2005).

The terms that describe and identify the elements of brand identity are often interpreted in various ways and used interchangeably (Urde, 2003). Also, it is difficult to classify them into definite categories due to the symbolic and dynamic nature of brand identity. Thus, narratives were analyzed and categorized according to the definition of the brand identity components and then realigned them to common theme and patterns.

IV. Data analysis

1. *Natural dream: iCOOP*

iCOOP aimed to supply safe and reliable products according to cooperatives principle and values (iCOOP, 2017). The concrete objectives of business that chief executives and working members unanimously declared are to provide safe food and realize principles and values of cooperatives, which is to pursue sustainable society through cooperation, complying with the principles like members' economic participation, democratic decision-making processes and transparency. iCOOP is seeking ways to raise social standards for food safety through consumer movement, such as 'complete labels of food' and 'anti-GMO', and to build a foundation for public participation (iCOOP, 2017).

> Cooperatives should not be perceived as an interest group that only seeks to members' interests. iCOOP contributes to the whole society through consumer movement and activities for public benefits. Such a campaign for 'complete labels of food' demanding the rights to know and information transparency would raise social standards. . . .
>
> Using cooperatives' store is also a way of participating in cooperatives' movement. iCOOP opened the opportunities to join in various ways like volunteering, campaigns, and management activities in local cooperatives. The values and philosophy of cooperatives are important; however, they should become a certain scale in numbers to attract social attention and to be a driving force for positive change.
>
> (interviewee D)

iCOOP believes that the ultimate goal is to change society through members' participation and its brand mission should be expanded to meet the needs and wants of members that change with the times. The mission statement enacted and declared for the 20th anniversary has expanded its business goals from food safety to whole life security, including care, education, housing and medical care (iCOOP, 2017).

> The needs and wants of members change with the times. Business must reflect the needs and wants of members. They used to want cheap but safe food before, but nowadays they want the best quality in taste and shape. iCOOP is striving to make products that consumers want, with technological development and cooperation with producers.
>
> (interviewee C)

> To solve today's problems such as infertility and atopic disease, safe environment as well as safe food are required. Therefore, the area of safe goods and services are likely to expand gradually.
>
> (interviewee A)

iCOOP wants to create a desirable future by focusing on reality and solving the current challenges one by one, based on the core values as 'the future building together, now and here'. Food safety campaigns as a way of practice aim to raise social interest and to organize public basis for change, and then the awareness of consumers and changes of consumption behavior will bring about changes in the way of production.

Producers would have the reason to change the way they produce when consumers demand.

(interviewee D)

It is a cooperative system and power that can transform the selfish desire into an altruistic desire; selfish desire like 'I want to be happy' into an altruistic desire like 'Everybody needs to live well in order for me to be happy and live well.

(interviewee B)

iCOOP has been practicing 'uniting business and decentralizing organization' since local cooperatives united together and established an association, and in this context, the organization name 'iCOOP' and the brand name 'Natural Dream' have been used separately. To clarify the business identity of eco-friendly products and enhance its value as a brand, iCOOP has adopted 'Natural Dream', meaning 'natural food that consumers want', as a brand name. iCOOP have been striving to provide consumers with the ideal products and services that guarantee not only safety but also high quality they want. Interviewee C said that the result of such efforts is alternative food like a cola with natural ingredients, chocolate without chemical additives, non-GMO pressed oil and Korean wheat gluten.

It is the consumer's power that makes alternative products such as Korean wheat gluten; previously gluten was only made of imported wheat, non-GMO pressed oil not using chemical additives to extract oil because consumers wanted and asked for the safe and high-quality products. It was something that other private distribution companies never try in that their purpose is to maximize profits. I think it was possible that iCOOP is a consumer-centered cooperative.

(interviewee D)

Interviewee B and D insisted that iCOOP is the only consumer-centered cooperative with consumers' view in this supplier-centered domestic distribution system. The brand vision is to expand its businesses up to more than 500 stores nationwide so that people who do not have any understanding of cooperatives would be able to participate in the cooperative movement anytime and anywhere. The ultimate purpose and vision of iCOOP are to make 'a happy world together' where nobody worries about child care and elderly care, jobs and economic inequality. iCOOP tries to serve as a base for social change as a desirable model of distribution and production and as a human-centered economic system.

'Let's live happily together' is what iCOOP wish for at last. iCOOP tries to build clusters and to create 'cooperative ecosystem', providing alternatives to live happily without competing in this market-oriented society.

(interviewee C)

I think a happy life is possible only if economic inequality is resolved. It would be possible when the wage gap is reduced and the social system is expanded where both producers and employees can get paid for their labor properly and enjoy the benefits of welfare. . . . Like Northern European countries where the gap between the rich and the poor is small, the national competitiveness is high, and the social safety net is well established so that there is no worry about education, care, and aging. That's what a happy life is and what we wish for.

(interviewee A)

The interviews are examined by brand identity components and repetitive phrases in the unit in Table 6.2. Most frequently mentioned and an important semantic unit is 'consumer-centered, consumer movement popularization'.

Table 6.2 iCOOP brand identity narratives

Narratives	Components	Semantic keywords
Safe food provision; most reliable products; relief in everyday life; consumer movement to change society	Mission	Safe and reliable food provision
Ethical consumerism; cooperation between consumers and producers; sustainable eco-friendly production oriented	Mission	Fulfillment of principles and values of cooperatives
Member investment·participation·operation; practice democracy; transparency; the most reliable cooperative	Mission	
Making the future together; Solving problems in daily life; honesty; trust	Core values	
Natural food that consumers want; safe and high-quality products	Brand meaning	Safe food and products
Korean wheat gluten; pressed canola oil; self-developed fructooligosaccharide; coke without chemical additives; alternative products	Brand Characteristics	Development·production·distribution of alternative products that meet the needs and wants of consumers
Consumer-centered cooperatives; meet the needs and wants of consumers	Brand Characteristics	
500 stores nationwide; accessibility and convenience; various cooperative movement from simple purchase to volunteer work	Vision	Consumers' convenience; cooperative movement as a daily life
Securing decent jobs; improvement of economic inequality; raise minimum wage standard; human-centered economic structure; desirable model of an alternative economy	Vision	Realization of human-centered economy
Happy world together; cooperative eco-system; well-established social safety net	Vision	Happy life living together

2. Hansalim

Hansalim, rooted in the Catholic foundation and the peasant movement, has been carrying out a 'life movement'. The idea of Hansalim is based on the belief that it would save all the living things due to the relatedness. Interviewee F said that Hansalim has begun from the point of relating one another among producers, consumers and individuals revealing themselves.

> It is a human nature that those who sell want to be paid more and those who buy want to pay less. . . . It was the start of business that consumers would take responsibility for rural farmers' life and farmers take responsibility for urban consumers' food by connecting one another despite different interests.
>
> (interviewee F)

Hansalim aims to provide reliable food based on the trust between producers and consumers, to support organic farming, thereby to increase the self-sufficiency of food and to reduce carbon gas emissions. Also, Hansalim includes the agenda of 'saving local community life' where everyday life of individuals takes place in order to respond to the changes and demands of the times. Consumers seek to solve local problems with activities like networking food-related organizations, healthy lunch for schools, and building solar power plants and daycare facilities for the young and old.

> When it is difficult for an individual to take responsibility for child care and caring for the parents, it would be very helpful for a lot of people to share the responsibilities of caring and make them into a cooperative business. Hansalim cannot provide alternatives or solutions in all areas, however, I think that Hansalim or other cooperatives movement is needed in areas linked to human survival such as food, energy, and care.
>
> (interviewee F)

Hansalim means 'live together' with a philosophical view that all things in the universe are connected and follows the principle of 'circle of life'. As the saying goes, 'a grain of rice has a universe in it,' a grain of rice needs a whole universe to ripen, such as sunlight, wind, earth and labor of farmers. It is a grain of rice that everyone needs to survive, has a work of life, and is connected to all the others (Hansalim Moim, 1989). Hansalim would not trade in any goods if they are against the philosophy and principles of it, even though they are useful for living. In other words, Hansalim does not deal with any goods that are harmful to the natural environment or labor environment, despite their usefulness and convenience.

> There was a demand from members for summer rayon comforter. Working members try to find the right manufacturers and the process of deliberation begun. Then they found that the process of extracting thread is difficult and rigorous and generates hazardous substances, so a lot of workers had been injured or died due to the poor labor circumstances. The board member decided not to handle the rayon products not only because of

the hazardous materials but also the workers who would be sacrificed in the production process.

(interviewee G)

One of the complaints from Hansalim members is that there are no cucumbers, peppers, zucchinis during winter and early spring at the stores. They grow when it's warm, thus heating facilities are needed. But we decided not to harm the environment just to get non-seasonable vegetables.

(interviewee E)

With the 30th anniversary (2017), Hansalim aims to expand the network of cooperation by widening and deepening its 'idea of life' (Hansalim Federation, 2017). It highlights its movement for self-reliance and care and presents new businesses and activities such as education, health care, finance and environment as its vision. The interviews are examined by brand identity components and repetitive phrases in the unit in Table 6.3.

Table 6.3 Hansalim brand identity narratives

Narratives	Components	Semantic keywords
Save food on the table-save lives-save local communities; reliable foods; increase food self-sufficiency rate; make organic agriculture sustainable; reduce carbon gas	Mission	The idea of life; the movement for life
Meet the needs through cooperation; members' participation; transparency	Mission	Fulfillment of the principles and values of cooperatives
Action from me; self-reflection; the circle of life; relation	Core values	The organic relationship among all the beings; trust; live together
Live together; save food; save all the living things; save local communities; preciousness of life	Brand meaning	
Philosophy starting from relationships; policies considering the process of production and environment; priorities of social values and principles; self-management; self-inspection; self-certification; pride and confidence in producers; cooperation among producers	Brand Characteristics	
Recovery of local communities; networking within the community; solidarity with local communities	Vision	Local communities
Shared space; expansion of goods and services; solve the problems of daily life through cooperation and relationship	Vision	Members' convenience; cooperative movement and participation as a daily life
Alternative models for food, energy, and care; retail system available to low-income households; sustainable circular society	Vision	Sustainable society

3. Dure

Dure aims to build a society where the value of life is respected and to bring together members, producers and local communities through cooperation and solidarity (Dure website). Dure is based on local cooperatives built by local residents to resolve their problems. To express its cooperative movement in accordance with Korean culture and sentiment, 'Dure', which means joint labor, was selected as the brand name.

> When we consider 'Rochdale pioneer cooperatives' as Korean culture, it is similar to a communal life of ancestors who tried to overcome difficulties. As we thought the process of overcoming difficulties was not only tough and depressing but also excited and hopeful, so we decided on the brand name in the hope that we would become such a community.
>
> (interviewees I and L)

The main feature of Dure is that its local cooperatives hold individuality and autonomous discretion. Local cooperatives that have long established relational values with local residents manage their activities on their own, and delegate business and logistics to the Dure association. In addition, they have the discretion to choose and sell local products to some extent. Their independent and autonomous local businesses could be a burden on the efficiency of operation, standard of goods and trust, but the positive factors are that the number of members is steadily increased, and the business is expanded so that care and nursing also come from the power of local cooperatives.

> Local cooperatives have established relationships with their members in the region, have also solved problems, and have built local communities. The Dure association can be seen as a business backup for them to do their works. So, the local cooperatives are highly autonomous and independent.
>
> (interviewee J)

Dure aims to create 'a better world' where the gap between the rich and the poor is resolved, and every person would be respected. The cooperatives movement would be justified and persuasive if members and consumers would recognize that the surplus of business is returned to the local community and used for a better life of the community. Table 6.4 shows Dure's brand identity and repetitive phrases in the unit.

> I wish 500,000 households, 3% of the total, would join the membership in ten years. As the number of members who experience cooperative movement is increasing, the social economy becomes stronger, and finally the world we dream of where the value of life and use are respected not the market-oriented value of exchange.
>
> (interviewee K)

Table 6.4 Dure brand identity narratives

Narratives	Components	Semantic keywords
Safe food; solve the needs and wants of local communities; the local circular economy of mutual cooperation	Mission	Provide safe food; fulfill the principles and values of cooperatives
Cooperation between producers and members; cooperation among members; regional solidarity; transparency	Mission	
Co-operation between producers and members, and among members	Core values	
Cheerful community; communities that overcome difficulties together; a spirit of sacrifice; local communities	Brand Meaning	Local communities
Autonomy and uniqueness of local cooperatives; local products; relational value in local communities	Brand Characteristics	Autonomy and uniqueness of local cooperatives
Stores to use conveniently; various goods and services to respond to the needs and wants of members; expand businesses from safe food to services such as care, mutual benefits, and welfare; address local problems	Vision	Members' convenience
Resolve the gap between the rich and the poor; make a better world by cooperation; become a foundation for the social economy; grow to 500,000 household members; an alternative economy where the value of life and use are respected	Vision	A better future; an alternative economy

4. *Happycoop*

Happycoop was established in order to solve various problems such as education, environment and women's rights and change the social system through direct trade between consumers and producers. Happycoop aims to (1) expand the collective power of consumers for eco-friendly and sustainable productions, (2) resolve problems of daily life, (3) create local communities where democracy is practiced and (4) build a society in which diversity is respected, as stated by 2017 business goals (Happycoop, 2017).

> I considered that movements for women's rights and gender equality are important and wanted to be a part of it. That's why I became a member of Happycoop and keep participating in its activities.
>
> (interviewee M)

Happycoop has provided for women with opportunities of education and gatherings to help them strengthen and grow their capacities, in which women are able to learn new values and culture and try to live happily. Here 'women' has a comprehensive meaning, including not only women but also the under-privileged, and 'living happily' refers to live their own life independently in the relations of harmony, cooperation and equality. In 2005, Happycoop tried to draw a picture of what to do in the daily lives of the cooperative movement and asked members what they wanted the most from the cooperative activities. The answer was 'happiness'.

> The answer 'happiness' comes out of the thought that what is the most precious thing to do and what is the most precious value to realize. What everybody wanted was not more democracy or more economic development but happiness.
>
> (interviewee O)

The word 'happiness' is abstract and can be understood in various ways, but Happycoop defined it as to 'live its own life independently' and to 'live together in cooperation with neighbors at the same time'. Happycoop has put the word 'happiness' for the title of newsletters and eventually used it for the brand name.

> If Happycoop was a men-centered organization, it would not be possible to use the term 'happiness'. Men usually are not drawn to that kind of word. It is a women-centered cooperative, so every member is able to express their feelings and thoughts honestly and accept them. Cooperatives is not a system or policy but people's movement. People have desires to help themselves and make their lives fulfilled, which makes them happy. Happycoop would be the place where the desires can be realized.
>
> (interviewee O)

> I wish Happycoop would play a role of supporting lives of the underprivi-leged and remain as a small but unique 'women-centered' cooperative.
>
> (interviewee M)

Happycoop supports women producers in rural areas in this context, helping people to live happily and live their own lives independently.

> There are many married farmers in rural areas, who work together to produce crops. But women are not respected or acknowledged as a farmer, and only the name of male producers are recorded in the products. Happycoop has made efforts to list all the names of couple producers on products and has been holding an overnight trip for women to provide them with a break and opportunity to talk about their difficulties. It has become a tradition that women producers look forward to.
>
> (interviewee M)

Table 6.5 Happycoop brand identity narratives

Narratives	Components	Semantic keywords
Safe and reliable eco-friendly food; provide daily goods to support women's life	Mission	Provide safe and reliable food;
Women's independent life; opportunities for women to strengthen and grow their capacities; the happiness of life	Mission	Support women's independent lives
Members' participation; discretion of local cooperatives; transparency	Mission	Fulfill the principles and values of cooperatives
Harmony (between nature and men), Cooperation (between men and men), Equality (between men and women, the disabled and not disabled)	Core values	Harmony, Cooperation, Equality
Spread happiness; try to change its own life to be independent and real	Brand Meaning	Happiness
Ecological sensitivity and delicacy of emotional caring of women; respect women producers and interact with them; women-centered; the power of an organization to engage and grow women	Brand Characteristics	Women-centered
Small but unique cooperative; women-centered; women's independent lives	Vision	
Desirable model of social economy; welfare system such as caring and mutual benefits; an alternative human-centered economy	Vision	Alternative human-centered economy

I am worried about how to get old in this era of aging. I wish women live their own lives independently, work in the local communities, and get along with friends as they get older. I hope Happycoop would provide various life models and cases for women in their 50s and 60s, which might be the future vision of Happycoop.

(interviewee O)

Table 6.5 shows the interviews by brand identity components and repetitive phrases in the unit.

V. Conclusion

There are common characteristics of brand identities in the four Korean consumer cooperatives such as 'supply of safe and reliable food', 'fulfillment of the principles and values of cooperatives' and 'realization of a human-centered alternative

Table 6.6 Common and different features of each cooperative

Features	Brand Identity	
Common features	Provide safe and reliable food	
	Fulfill the principles and values of cooperatives	
	Realize the human-centered alternative economy	
Different features	iCOOP	Popularize cooperative movement through consumer-centered consumer movement
	Hansalim	Save all living things, reveal individual beings through their relationships
	Dure	Independent and autonomous local community
	Happycoop	Support women's independent lives

economy'. The background and orientation of each cooperative were different, but they built common brand identity in that all of them seek alternatives in the specific living area, such as safe food in the 1980s when economic, social and political changes took place (Kim, 2014; Hwang, 2015).

On the other hand, the differences among them are mainly found in the core values and characteristics. Based on the core value of 'making a future together', iCOOP has a strategy to look at issues of daily living from the consumers' perspectives and lead a 'consumer-centered consumer movement'. Hansalim aims to 'save all living things' as its mission and values 'organic relationships of all beings'. Dure has the vision to play a key role to solve social problems with the residents by making the most of independence and autonomy of local cooperatives. Happycoop, rooted in 'Women's Link' showed a distinct brand identity as 'women-centered', supporting women's happiness and independent lives.

This chapter identified the brand identity of each consumer cooperative and found common and distinct features among them, which could be a strategic basis of marketing. In contrast to corporations, cooperatives are usually a lack of capital and human power to invest in marketing and brand management. However, cooperatives can build brand identity with consistent and clear messages such as mission, vision and core values, and raise the dedication and loyalty of members by delivering them through products and services.

References

Aaker, D. A. (1992) 'The Value of Brand Equity.' *Journal of Business Strategy*, 13(4): 27–32.
Aaker, D. A. (1996) *Building Strong Brands*. New York, NY: Free Press.
Beverland, M. (2007) 'Can Cooperatives Brand? Exploring the Interplay Between Cooperative Structure and Sustained Brand Marketing Success.' *Food Policy*, 32(4): 480–495.

Brown, A. D. (2006) 'A Narrative Approach to Collective Identities.' *Journal of Management Studies*, 43(4): 731–753.

Chang, W. S., and Lee, J. E. (2009) 'The Performance and Problems of Consumers' Cooperatives in Korea.' *Journal of Korean Society for Cooperative Studies*, 27(1): 179–201.

Chreim, S. (2005) 'The Continuity–Change Duality in Narrative Texts of Organizational Identity.' *Journal of Management Studies*, 42(3): 567–593.

Collins, J. C., and Porras, J. I. (1996) 'Building Your Company's Vision.' *Harvard Business Review*, 74(5): 65.

Cooper, P. (1999) 'Consumer Understanding, Change and Qualitative Research.' *International Journal of Market Research*, 41(1): 1.

Creswell, J. W. (2007) *Qualitative Inquiry & Research Design: Choosing among Five Approaches*. Thousand Oaks, CA: Sage Publications, Inc.

De Chernatony, L. (1999) 'Brand Management Through Narrowing the Gap Between Brand Identity and Brand Reputation.' *Journal of Marketing Management*, 15(1–3): 157–179.

De Chernatony, L., and Cottam, S. (2006) 'Internal Brand Factors Driving Successful Financial Services Brands.' *European Journal of Marketing*, 40(5/6): 611–633.

De Chernatony, L., Harris, F., and Dall'Olmo Riley, F. (2000) 'Added Value: Its Nature, Roles and Sustainability.' *European Journal of Marketing*, 34(1/2): 39–56.

Dure Consumer Cooperatives (2017) *Je 20cha Jung-gi Dae-ui-won Chong-hoe-ja-ryo-jip* [20th General Assembly Report]. Dure Consumer Cooperatives (eds.). Unpublished Report. Seoul, Korea: Dure.

Grace, D., and O'Cass, A. (2005) 'Examining the Effects of Service Brand Communications on Brand Evaluation.' *Journal of Product & Brand Management*, 14(2): 106–116.

Gurley, D. K., Peters, G. B., Collins, L., and Fifolt, M. (2015) 'Mission, Vision, Values, and Goals: An Exploration of Key Organizational Statements and Daily Practice in Schools.' *Journal of Educational Change*, 16(2): 217–242.

Hansalim Federation (2017) *Je-7cha Jung-gi Chong-hoe-ja-ryo-jip* [7th General Assembly Report]. Seoul, Korea: Hansalim Federation.

Hansalim Moim (1989) *Hansalim Seon-eon* [Hansalim Declaration]. Seoul, Korea: Hansalim.

Happycoop (2017) *Je-7cha Dae-eui-won Chong-hoe-ja-ryo-jip* [Assembly Report for Delegates]. Unpublished Report. Seoul, Korea: Happycoop.

Hardesty, S. D. (2005) 'Cooperatives as Marketers of Branded Products.' *Journal of Food Distribution Research*, 36(1): 237–242.

Harris, F., and de Chernatony, L. (2001) 'Corporate Branding and Corporate Brand Performance.' *European Journal of Marketing*, 35(3/4): 441–456.

Harris, L. C., and Goode, M. M. (2004). 'The Four Levels of Loyalty and the Pivotal Role of Trust: A Study of Online Service Dynamics.' *Journal of Retailing*, 80(2): 139–158.

Hastings, K., and Perry, C. (2000) 'Do Services Exporters Build Relationships? Some Qualitative Perspectives.' *Qualitative Market Research: An International Journal*, 3(4): 207–214.

He, H., Li, Y., and Harris, L. (2012) 'Social Identity Perspective on Brand Loyalty.' *Journal of Business Research*, 65(5): 648–657.

Hwang, J. A. (2015) 'Hyupdong-eui Poong-kyung: iCOOP Saeng hyup johapwon-deul-eui sangho yi-ik gyeong-hum-eul batangeuro' [The Scene of Cooperation: iCOOP Consumer Cooperative Members' Practices of Ethical Consumption and Construction of 'Hyeopyeoan']. *Cooperatives Network*, 68: 95–123.

iCOOP Union (2017) *Je-19-cha Dae-eui-won Chong-hoe-ja-ryo-jip* [19th General Assembly Report for Delegates]. Unpublished Report. Seoul: iCOOP.

Jensen, M. C., and Meckling, W. H. (1979) 'Rights and Production Functions: An Application to Labor-managed Firms and Codetermination.' *Journal of business*, 52(4): 469–506.

Jeong, E. M. (2006) 'Saeng-hwal Hyup-dong-jo-hap-ui Teug-seong' [Characteristics of Consumers' Cooperatives in Korea]. *Journal of Rural Development*, 29(3): 1–18.

Kapferer, J. N. (2012) *The New Strategic Brand Management: Advanced Insights and Strategic Thinking*. London: Kogan Page.

Keller, K. L. (2001) *Building Customer-Based Brand Equity: A Blueprint for Creating Strong Brands*. Cambridge, MA: Marketing Science Institute.

Keller, K. L., and Lehmann, D. R. (2006) 'Brands and Branding: Research Findings and Future Priorities.' *Marketing Science*, 25(6): 740–759.

Kim, G. S. (2014) *Kkae-eo-na-la! Hyup-dong-jo-hap* [Wake up! Cooperatives!]. First Edition. Paju, Korea: Deul-nyeok.

Kim, I. S. (2012) 'Hang-bok Jung-sim Saenghyup, Saeroun Baldoteum-ae Bak-soo-reul' [HappyCoop, Applause for a New Start]. Ham-kye-ga-neun Yeo-sung [Women Going Together]. *Minwoohoe* [Woomenlink], 209: 42–43.

Kim, Y. C. (2013) *Jiljeok yeongoo bang-beop-ron I: Bricoleur* [Qualitative Research Methodology I: Bricoleur]. Second Edition. Seoul, Korea: Academy Press.

Kwon, O. B. (2012) 'Hankook Hyup-dong-johap woon-dong-eui sung-kwa, i-nyeom, chun-mang' [Korean Consumer's Cooperative Movement: Performance, Idea, Prospect]. *Journal of Social Science*, 18(2): 139–158.

Lee, C. S., Kim, R. S., and Kim, Y. R. (2015) *2015 Hyup-dong-johap Sil-tae-josa* [A Study on Cooperatives Status in 2015]. Hankook Bogunsahoe Yeongoowon [Korea Institute for Health and Social Affairs]. Seoul, Korea: Ministry of Economy & Finance.

Lee, G. N. (2013) 'Saeng-hwal Hyup-dong-jo-hap-eui Gyeong-je-jeok Yeok-hal-bun-seok' [Review on Function of Consumer Cooperatives–Price Level and Volatility of Eco-Friendly Agricultural Products]. *Studies on Consumer Affairs*, 44(1): 179–196.

Nandan, S. (2005) 'An Exploration of the Brand Identity-Brand Image Linkage: A Communications Perspective.' *Journal of Brand Management*, 12(4): 264–278.

Novkovic, S. (2008) 'Defining the Co-operative Difference.' *The Journal of Socio-Economics*, 37(6): 2168–2177.

Schein, E. H. (2010) *Organizational Culture and Leadership*. Hoboken, NJ: John Wiley & Sons.

Seo, I. D. (2014) *Yugigagong-sikpoom Brand Identity Yeongoo: Saenghwal Hyup-dong-jo-hap Hansalim brand Joong-sim-eu-ro* [Study on the Brand Identity Design Development of Organic Process Food-Focused on Cooperative Society 'Hansa-lim']. Master Dissertation. Seoul: Ewha Womans University.

Shin, S. S. (2011) *Saeroun saeng-hyup woon-dong-eui mirae* [The Future of Cooperatives Movement]. Seoul, Korea: Purun Namu.

Upshaw, L. B. (1995). *Building Brand Identity: A Strategy for Success in a Hostile Marketplace*. New York: Wiley.

Urde, M. (2003) 'Core Value-Based Corporate Brand Building.' *European Journal of Marketing*, 37(7/8): 1017–1040.

Wheeler, A. (2003). *Designing Brand Identity: A Complete Guide to Creating, Building, and Maintaining Strong Brands*. New York: John Wiley & Sons.

Zaltman, G. (1997) 'Rethinking Market Research: Putting People Back In.' *Journal of Marketing Research*, 34(4): 424–437.

Websites

Dure Cooperatives. http://dure-coop.or.kr/.
Hansalim Cooperatives. http://www.hansalim.or.kr/.
Happycoop Cooperatives. http://www.happycoop.or.kr/.
iCOOP Cooperatives. http://www.icoop.or.kr/.

7 Member participation and productivity changes

Sunyoung Jung and Woosuk Choi

I. Introduction

During the 1980s to 1990s, consumer cooperatives in Korea were organized in order to ensure producers steady economic activities and provide consumers the provision of non-harmful products; they have also promoted the direct trade of eco-friendly agricultural foods. In 1999, the Consumer Cooperative Act was enacted and then the revised one was legislated in 2000, based on which consumer cooperatives actively diversified their products and constructed associations. Such activities have consequently enhanced management efficiency through multi-faced management. The Framework Act on Cooperative was formed in 2012, and there have been more than 10,000 cooperatives established since then.

The strategy that consumer cooperatives in the late 1990s opted for was associations (or solidarity). Some local consumer cooperatives formed an association in order to solve the problems they faced. They reorganized the distribution system more effectively, enhanced the economic efficiency and succeeded in expanding the number of members and planning the business stability at the same time through organizing the associations. It corresponds with the research by Kim et al. (2016) that building the cooperation process would generate new opportunities and values within organizations. Consequently, the era of 10,000 cooperatives was motivated by the historical experience of solidarity.

Consumer cooperatives have overcome the crisis in a way most appropriate to their ultimate purpose is crucial to those who participate in the cooperative movement. Nevertheless, the management principle of cooperative cannot be explained by the dichotomous perspective of market and firm because of the dual nature that a cooperative is an association and also a member-owned firm (Valentinov, 2004). Firm theories can be applied to analyze most parts of the nature of the enterprise. However, 'social interests' that cooperatives create and 'the achievement of common good' that they pursue could be withdrawn from consideration when evaluating their performance within the frame of the mainstream firm theories (Argandona, 1998). It is because the mainstream firm theories explain the nature of firms through the core concepts such as 'contract' and 'competence' but do not take into account in what ways they should be managed.

The purposes of this chapter are twofold. Firstly, this study will show that, based on cooperative theories, there are other types of performance that cannot be measured with mainstream theories. Secondly, it will analyze the relationships between member participation and changes in productivity of consumer cooperatives on the basis of the fact that solidarity between local cooperatives during the 1997 Financial Crisis in Korea appears as member participation within each cooperative.

This chapter analyses differences between the mainstream theory of the firms and the theories dealing with cooperative by reviewing both perspectives. Then, it examines changes in productivity and causes of such changes observed in 'Hansalim consumer cooperative' using their financial and non-financial indicators. Hansalim is a consumer cooperative that deals in eco-friendly agricultural foods, processed products and daily supplies, and seven district branches that were run during the study period from 2012 to 2016 are selected as the unit of analysis of productivity change.

Data and materials analyzed include the annual reports of the branches, and reports of the board of directors, and the member activity department and the management strategy department. The Malmquist output-based productivity index using DEA (Data Envelopment Analysis) is employed as an analysis method. Judging the performance of the cooperative by a single factor such as financial indicator is not reasonable, so the method that can analysis productivity using multiple inputs and outputs are employed. With this method, especially, a non-financial indicator is available, which cannot be substituted by monetary values.

II. Theoretical background and literature review

1. The theory of the firms and cooperative

Foss (1993) suggests the theories of the firms, dividing it into two perspectives: contractual and competence perspectives. These two approaches show differences between the boundary of firms and their competitive relations. First of all, the theory of the firms from the contractual perspective is summarized as follows. Traditionally, the complete competitive market defined by economics is based on interaction without contract cost or other expenses. In 1937, however, Coase raises a doubt as to the 'frictionless world' by the neo-classical school and suggests a world in which there are market coordination costs or transaction costs. In other words, he highlights 'marketing cost' that is inevitable when trading in the market and reveals the reason why firms exist.

Since then, scholars such as Alchian and Demsetz (1972), Williamson (1975) have supported and developed Coase's argument. The focal points of the theory of transaction costs they argue are as follows: first, a perfect long-term contract is impossible since trade actors cannot predict the future and, after the contract, there could be re-negotiation followed by extra costs and exhausting actions; second, when there is 'relationship-specific investments', vertical integration into a unitary firm is more efficient than trade through contract; third, the negotiation between individual firms is replaced to 'authority' after the vertical integration (Hart, 2011). Furthermore, Grossman and Hart (1986), who emphasize rights generated during the contract, divide the rights into 'specific rights' and 'residual rights'. And they also argue that specifying the requirements to fulfill within the initial contract costs a lot; therefore, one of the actors own the residual rights in order to overcome the incompleteness of the contract, which is defined as 'ownership'. They ultimately explain why transaction in the market has transformed into firms and in what ways authority within firms is intensified.

The other perspective of the theory of the firms is related to competence. The classical definition of competence is created by Selznick (1997), and he defines distinctive competence as 'the set of activities that an organization could perform especially well in relation to its competitors'. Also, Hamel and Prahalad (1990) explain competence as the collective learning in the organization, especially the capacity to coordinate diverse production skills and integrate streams of technologies. The firm theories from the competence perspective consider 'skill' of individuals or teams that is advanced and sustained through the organization and 'tacit knowledge' as the core concepts (Hodgson, 1998). The theories that put emphasis on the competence of firms have more various points of view than those that regard the contract as the nature of firms. Knight (1921) is a scholar who has played an outstanding role in suggesting the competence perspective theories and draws attention to 'uncertainty' as well as knowledge, saying that uncertainty is a crucial factor to explain the existence of firms. According to him, thus, it is a key factor of management to solve problems caused by the uncertainty of members' opinions or behaviors. After Knight's argument, competence is explained as the set of productive opportunities by Penrose (1959) and as a repository of productive knowledge by Winter (1988). To summarize, the competence perspective focuses on the dynamic side of firms, considering training, innovation and sustaining competitive advantage significant, and also the role of entrepreneurs to control them. Additionally, it explains that cumulated productive competence according to each firm's experiences in history decides the heterogeneous nature of firms as it sees a firm as a set of productive resources (Foss, 1993).

A fundamental idea applied when explaining why cooperatives are not replaced by capitalistic organizations is that there are interdependencies between economic actors and different governances are needed depending on them (Valentinov, 2004). Although the concept of economic interdependence is still controversial to a great extent, interdependencies are inevitable, as economic actors generally need 'acknowledged economic resources' to use in economic activities. The acknowledged economic resources can be divided into three types: when economic actors can use the resources as they need, when they cannot use nor obtain them in any way and when they cannot use the resources as many as they need but obtain the rest amount through interaction with other economic actors. Especially, the last case is where economic interdependencies occur and, in this case, cooperating organizational structure based on social capital is seen as the most adequate. Therefore, the cooperative strategy on the basis of member participation can be effective when there are symmetrical interdependencies. Explaining the governance of the organization with symmetrical interdependencies between internal performers results in an analysis of the cause of cooperation without the use of transaction cost theory. If the symmetrical interdependency is valuable in reality, trades with such a characteristic do not have to be run through the capitalist market or hierarchical mechanism.

Member participation is most important in order for symmetrical interdependencies to work seamlessly. Thus, factors that encourage members to participate need to be scrutinized. In relation to this, Birchall and Simmons (2004) introduce member participation in cooperatives and a participation strategy by 'mutual incentive theory'. Basically, the incentive theory is divided into two: individualistic motivation derived from social exchange theory and collective motivation originated from cooperation theory. The former says that individuals are motivated depending on rewards and punishments, on the other hand, the latter argues that motivations can be generated due to shared values, shared goals and a sense of community. Mutual incentive theory focuses on the latter, rather than the former.

As suggested by mutual incentive theory, the fact that member participation can be encouraged by shared values, shared goals and sense of community has a significant meaning to cooperative management. When the scale of cooperative is enlarged and member participation is realized through the board of directors, member participation could exist merely formally. There is not a clearly defined relationship between the scale of cooperative and member participation; it is necessary for consumer cooperatives that have been increasing in scale to consider such an issue. Hence, it is noteworthy that Hansalim has tried to subdivide the organization into smaller units as their scale increases, such as providing their members with opportunities to participate in the management and activities through establishing local organizations.

The firm theories from the contractual perspective that were looked through above are seen as advanced in terms of explicating the nature of firms, departing from microeconomic theory defining firms as 'black box'. Having said that, a limit of the contractual perspective theories is observed from the fact that they figure out the best contractual form and the greatest level of monitoring under the supposition that there are inputs, production and producing technologies, and such a fixed conceptualization leads to the limited understanding of firms as static organizations. In addition, these theories adhere to 'contract', which makes them pursue cooperation in a superficial form. In contrast, cooperatives that put cooperation and solidarity before anything, as their critical values are considered as having the internal factor to trigger cooperation (Park et al., 2015).

Table 7.1 The firm theories and cooperative

	Contract-perspective firm theories	Competence-perspective firm theories	Cooperative
Purpose of the firm	Minimize transaction costs (Coase, 1937)	Develop productive capabilities (Penrose, 1959)	Needs and desire of members
Nature of the firm	Nexus of contracts (Alchian and Demsetz, 1972)	Repository of productive knowledge (Winter, 1988)	Interdependency
Core cost	Transaction costs	Information and production costs	Adjustment costs
Interaction structure within firm	Negotiation (incentives)	Adjustment	Commitment

Although the firm theories with the competence perspective assume that cooperatives would fail in adjusting decision making, Thompson (2015) suggests that cooperatives can achieve successful adjustment through cooperation without adverse selection, which is possible due to the characteristic of cooperative governance. If cooperative members can establish a comparably great level of agreement and trust, there would be less violation of the regulation. There are actually some cooperatives that are highly productive with a few observers and profit shares (Kruse, 1993). Also, cooperatives accumulate knowledge in the community through cooperation so as to fulfill their members' needs and desires and run their businesses by utilizing the collective knowledge they own. It can be said that the cooperative is the best form of business organization that includes the productivity of capital that Veblen (1908) suggests.

2. Data Envelopment Analysis (DEA) – Malmquist productivity analysis

1) Efficiency and productivity

One of the most noticeable ways to measure the performance of organizations or institutions is efficiency or productivity measurement. From the economic point of view, efficiency refers to Pareto efficiency, but it means the ratio of best input to values of reached outputs or performances when measuring performances. Therefore, what efficiency really means is 'relative efficiency' because efficiency and inefficiency are compared based on an organizational unit that has achieved the best practice.

Productivity, unlike efficiency, refers to output values divided by input values (Lee and Oh, 2012). Productivity change is measured by looking at how the ratio of output to input is changed according to the time change. In terms of including technical change as well as technical efficiency, productivity can be differentiated from efficiency (Yoo, 2002).

In general, there are two ways of measuring productivity: one is to measure single factor productivity and the other total factor productivity (i.e. multifactor productivity). Mostly, single factor productivity is measured rather than the other due to its measurability, but there is a limit to measuring productivity efficiency by single factor productivity. It is because output depends on reciprocal actions between various input factors. In contrast, total factor productivity explains the relation between total input factors and outputs, which is normally defined as output per unit of capital and labor combined. The rise of productivity through a change in total factor productivity appears as a shift of production function and the shift seems to work corresponding to technical change and the rest such as qualitative improvement of the workforce, management innovation, change of organizational culture and so on. Hence, the increase of total factor productivity can be interpreted into an overall technical change in the production process and rise of efficiency.

2) DEA

DEA is an efficiency analysis method firstly suggested by Charnes, Cooper, and Rhodes in 1978 who incorporated the non-parametric efficiency measurement and the distance function demonstrated by Farrell (1957) and provided the formulation with a supposition of constant returns to scale. Subsequently, Banker et al. (1984) subdivided technical efficiency into pure technical efficiency and scale efficiency on the basis of variable returns to scale.

DEA, as a way of LP (Linear Programming), analyses relative efficiency by using input and output materials that constitute a production possibility set and then deducing EES (Empirical Efficient Surface). EES here indicates the most efficient frontier that optimizes resource allocation and maximizes productivity. A DMU (decision-making unit) placed on the frontier is considered efficient and, if not, it is regarded as inefficient. After that, the distance between the most efficient frontier and others is measured to grasp relative efficiency (Charnes et al., 1978).

DEA can apply varied patterns according to the property of materials to examine. Generally, DEA patterns can be changed depending on whether the production relation between input and output is constant returns to scale or variable returns to scale, and whether it is input-based or output-based when examining efficiency.

There are three types of efficiency calculated by DEA. Firstly, technical efficiency refers to the physical relationship between resources such as labor, materials and equipment and health outcome. It is concerned with achieving maximum outputs with the least cost. Next, allocative efficiency indicates how different resource inputs are combined to produce the mix of different outputs at an output level where the price equals the marginal cost of production, with an assumption that the organization has fulfilled technical efficiency entirely. Lastly, cost efficiency is a combination of the first and the second and it can be said to be cost-efficient when both efficiencies are achieved.

Advantages of DEA are as follows. Firstly, it is capable of handling multiple inputs and outputs, especially those that cannot be replaced by monetary values. Secondly, there is no need to explicitly specify a mathematical form for the production function as to inputs and outputs. Thirdly, decision-making units are directly compared against a peer or combination of peers. Fourthly, input and output factors can have different measurement units. In contrast, there are some disadvantages as well. It is sensitive to the selection of inputs and outputs. In addition, all probable errors are deemed as inefficiency errors. Also, it measures inefficiency based on relative efficiency rather than connecting the performance of observed value with statistical standard value.

3) Malmquist productivity index and precedent research

Malmquist productivity index measures the change of TFP (total factor productivity) of the research object using panel data. The change of TFP is measured by calculating technical efficiency change and technical change. Also, technical efficiency change is divided into pure technical efficiency change and scale efficiency change (Färe et al., 1994).

The current study uses the Malmquist output-based productivity index to measure technical efficiency change, technical change, pure technical efficiency change and scale efficiency change of Hansalim Seoul. In the research periods (2012–2016), the output-based productivity between period and period is defined as equation (1) (Färe et al., 1994).

$$M_o^{t+1}(x^{t+1},y^{t+1},x^t,y^t)=\left[\frac{D_o^t(x^{t+1},y^{t+1})}{D_o^t(x^t,y^t)}\times\frac{D_o^{t+1}(x^{t+1},y^{t+1})}{D_o^{t+1}(x^t,y^t)}\right]^{\frac{1}{2}} \qquad (1)$$

In equation (1), M_o indicates Malmquist productivity index (i.e. index of alteration of TFP), and $D_o^t(x^{t+1},y^{t+1})$ means the distance between the compared time $t+1$, and the reference point t. M_o = 1 refers to no change in productivity between the periods. If this index exceeds unity, it means an improvement in productivity, and values less than 1 suggest the converse. The equation (1) can be further decomposed into two components: change of technical efficiency and technical change (equation (2)).

$$M_o^{t+1}(x^{t+1},y^{t+1},x^t,y^t)=\frac{D_o^{t+1}(x^{t+1},y^{t+1})}{D_o^t(x^t,y^t)}$$
$$\times\left[\frac{D_o^t(x^{t+1},y^{t+1})}{D_o^{t+1}(x^{t+1},y^{t+1})}\times\frac{D_o^t(x^t,y^t)}{D_o^{t+1}(x^t,y^t)}\right]^{\frac{1}{2}} \qquad (2)$$

The first component in equation (2) means the change of technical efficiency. When putting the first component as E and the second one, which refers to technical change, T, the productivity index can be calculated as follows: M = E × T. The change in efficiency shows the same ratio as the technical efficiency of Farrell (1957) over the two time periods, t and $t + 1$. Also, the second component in equation (2) means the geometric mean of technical change between t and $t + 1$. The calculated value greater than unity indicates technical advance, and one less than unity means technical regression. The change of technical efficiency (E) can be decomposed into pure technical efficiency and scale efficiency, which is described as equation (3).

$$
\begin{aligned}
M_o^{t+1}(x^{t+1}, y^{t+1}, x^t, y^t) = {} & \frac{D_v^{t+1}(x^{t+1}, y^{t+1})}{D_v^T(x^t, y^t)} \\
& \times \left[\frac{D_c^{t+1}(x^{t+1}, y^{t+1}) / D_v^{t+1}(x^{t+1}, y^{t+1})}{D_c^t(x^t, y^t) / D_v^t(x^t, y^t)} \right] \\
& \times \left[\frac{D_c^t(x^{t+1}, y^{t+1})}{D_c^{t+1}(x^{t+1}, y^{t+1})} \times \frac{D_c^t(x^t, y^t)}{D_c^{t+1}(x^t, y^t)} \right]^{\frac{1}{2}}
\end{aligned}
\tag{3}
$$

The first and second components of equation (3), indicating pure technical efficiency and scale efficiency each, are based on VRS, and technical change is on the basis of CRS. Therefore, the Malmquist productivity index reflects the combination of efficiency change and technical change over time (Yoo, 2005).

Hong and Koo (2000) analyzed the productivity efficiency of 50 credit cooperatives in Seoul applying DEA in 1999. The inputs were the number of staff, size of the business place, and expenses and the outputs included new deposits, a new loan, deposit, loan, and business profits. The analysis has revealed that the majority of cooperatives with a management assessment second rating was inefficiently managed, and a few cooperatives with a management assessment third rating were efficiently run. Hong et al. (2002) conducted research between 1997 and 2002 on the efficiency change of 200 local credit cooperatives using the Malmquist productivity index. Deposit, labor costs and fixed assets were selected as inputs and loan and marketable securities as outputs. This research has shown that the local credit cooperatives were experiencing constantly decreasing productivity, which resulted from a decrease in technical efficiency.

In a study by Yoo (2002), the Malmquist productivity index changes of 89 local public enterprises with water service were measured using their panel data from 1997 to 2000. As a result of the study, the pure technical efficiency of the waterworks was improved since the financial crisis, but there was also scale inefficiency to some extent. Oh (2010) was on the management efficiency of the fisheries cooperative between 2004 and 2008. The inputs included the number of stores, the number of staff and equity and the outputs sales, business profits and deposit. There was a decreasing tendency in the efficiency of the fisheries cooperatives over time, and the efficient DMU and the inefficient DMU co-existed.

Choi et al. (2003) analyzed the management efficiency of 50 branches in the credit business sector of the National Federation of Fisheries Cooperatives. The number of staffs, project costs and fixed assets were the inputs and the outputs consisted of new profits, a new loan, deposit, loan and business profits. Compared to the average efficiency in 1999, the management efficiency in 2000 and 2001 have shown improvement. Jang (2011) carried out DEA and MPI analysis on 23 Hanaro Mart stores in Seoul from 2005 to 2009 and used the size of the store, the number of staff and the number of POS terminal as the inputs and the daily average customers and sales as the outputs. His study suggested the increase of scale efficiency is necessary for the efficiency of the Agricultural cooperative Hanaro Mart to increase. Kim (2014) researched the eco-efficiency and the business performance of 23 listed manufacturing companies in Korea using DEA. It was concluded that companies with good management of the environmental system and the high eco-efficiency through innovative environmental technologies showed better financial performance.

Ferrier (1994) carried out research comparing the technical efficiency and the scale efficiency of a dairy products private company and cooperatives in the United States, and examined the influence the attenuated rights of cooperative ownership have on productive efficiency. The output variable was the value of the shipment and the input variables unit labor value and capital. The results showed that the cooperatives' management was more efficient than that of private corporates in terms of technical efficiency and their scale efficiencies were at a similar level.

Färe et al. (1994) studied the productivity change of Swedish public medial institutions from 1970 to 1985 through non-radical Malmquist productivity index, which revealed the general flow of medical business productivity and the pattern of productivity change of each medical institution. The actual labors (four types of labor) for inputs and short-term inpatients, long-term inpatients and outpatients for outputs were selected in this research.

Barros and Santos (2007) analyze the productivity of cooperatives and 27 private companies in the Portuguese wine industry. Panel data between 1996 and 2000 were used for productivity analysis. The inputs included labor costs, the number of full-time employees and amortization and the outputs consisted of total sales, production and gross value added. It has shown that Portuguese wine cooperatives achieved a higher efficiency than the private companies, which seems to have resulted from the original factors of internal resources of cooperatives such as ownership and distribution structure from the resource-based perspective.

Guzman and Arcas (2008) employed the DEA method to measure management efficiency and the technical efficiency of 247 cooperatives in the Spanish agricultural sector. They selected fixed assets, labor costs, raw material costs, management costs and so on as inputs and sales as output. It has been proved that cooperatives in the agricultural sector should reach a certain standard in scale to obtain efficiency.

Posadas and Cabanda (2011) scrutinized the management performance of 117 electronic power cooperatives in 15 local areas of the Philippines. They have observed that the technical efficiency was obtained through technical innovation, applying the number of employees, power production costs, depreciation costs, operating costs, and general costs as inputs, and operating margin, the number of consumers, total assets, and sold wattage as outputs.

III. Research method

1. Hansalim Seoul

This research examines Hansalim Seoul consumer cooperative. Hansalim was initiated by Park Jae-Il, who opened 'Hansalim Farm' in Jaegi-dong, Seoul, in 1986, and has since grown as a nationwide organization. Hansalim Farm attempted direct trade between producers and consumers in 1986, established a consumer cooperative in 1988, and became incorporated based on the Consumer Cooperative Act in 1999. In 2002, it created Hansalim National Distribution Business Association and a distribution association. Thereafter, local organizations have been transformed into consumer cooperatives after several attempts, a united distribution system has become incorporated and the national movement body has formed a corporation. Finally, they launched Hansalim Association in 2011, which is owned by local consumer cooperatives. Depending on the local cooperatives, the degree of integration with the association is decided and there are three categories of integration (Table 7.2).

In 2003 Hansalim launched Hansalim Seoul consumer cooperative at their 16th general meeting in order to prepare the base of Hansalim movement in the metropolitan area. After several reorganizations, Hansalim Seoul has been divided into 8 regional branches. As of 2016, the regional branches include 72 local stores, and each branch runs the product supply business, participating in member activities at the same time. Moreover, the branches are founding local

Table 7.2 Types of integration of local Hansalim

Types	Integrating part	Range of integration	Notes
Type 1	Entire integration	Entire system	Invention and supply of local independent items
Type 2	Partial integration	Selective joint use of products	Utilizing part of data processing or distribution system
Type 3	Integration on demand	Joint use based on products	Selective utilization of products needed

organizations, which are a smaller unit than the branch. It was to encourage members to voluntarily participate in activities by constructing the organic organization that consists of 'headquarter-branch-local unit' according to the reorganization regulation of Hansalim Seoul in 2014. As of 2016, there are 8 local organizations that are running, and 17 pre-organizations are preparing meetings in order to become local organizations.

2. Input and output

Performance and outcomes generated by cooperative do not necessarily mean economic performance, so it is important to look through various indicators that highlight the value and performance of cooperative in order to measure productivity change of Hansalim Seoul properly. As there has been discussion over issues recently as to corporate social responsibility and sustainable development, non-financial indicators such as environment, society, labor, human right, governance and so on receive attention, which can be assessed through Triple Bottom Line concept. The Co-operative UK also emphasizes the societal performance of cooperatives as a core factor of sustainability of cooperatives and provides a specified means to measure performance, Simply Performance.

This research reflects variables applied in the precedent studies and the indicators used to measure financial, non-financial performances and sustainability, defined by the Co-operative UK in the selection of inputs and outputs. Inputs applied for productivity analysis of Hansalim Seoul are the number of members of each relevant branch.

The rationale of the selections of inputs is that it is judged that, in the case of cooperative, members' economic and management participation would significantly influence financial and non-financial performances. Especially, the number of members is calculated as precisely as possible by excluding withdrawn members every year.

Table 7.3 Inputs and outputs for Hansalim Seoul productivity analysis

List of variables	
Inputs	– The number of members
	– The number of participative members in management and activities (branch management meetings, local organization management meetings, subdivision meetings, town meetings, small meetings, store meetings, new stores meetings and urban-rural interchange included)
	– Labor (labor costs of activists and executives)
Outputs	– Sales
	– Reusable bottles collection rate
	– Farmland contribution area

Sales that are used as output are a generally used category when measuring financial performance. However, the farmland contribution area and the reusable bottle collection rate make it possible to see the sustainability performance of Hansalim Seoul. The farmland area contributed by Hansalim accounts for a very small proportion compared to the whole arable land in Korea. Nonetheless, rising quantities of primary produce and processed products to supply as consumption through consumer cooperatives increases would lead to the necessity to gradually expand the eco-friendly agricultural product cultivation area, in which Hasalim's farmland contribution could play a crucial role. Also, the expansion of the cultivation area is seen as critical sustainability performance in terms of preventing pollution of land and agricultural water and maintaining biodiversity. The reusable bottle collection rate is chosen as a non-financial performance for similar reasons, such as saving energy and reducing the amount of waste disposal.

3.   *Malmquist productivity index*

We calculate the distance functions that constitute the Malmquist index as a solution to linear programming problems. We assume that there are $k=1,. \ldots ,$ K observations of $n=1,. \ldots ,$ N inputs $x_n^{k,t}$ in each period $t=1,. \ldots ,$ T, which are employed to produce $k=1,. \ldots ,$ K observations of $m=1,. \ldots ,$ M outputs denoted $y_m^{k,t}$ in each period $t=1,. \ldots ,$ T. We assume that the number of observations does not change over time, where $\lambda^{k,t}$ is an intensity variable, familiar from activity analysis. These intensity variables serve to form the convex combinations of observed inputs and outputs, thus forming the technology or reference set. Next, suppose we wish to measure the relative productivity change of observation k between period t and period $t+1$.

$$D_o^t(x^{k,t}, y^{k,t}) = \min_{\theta, \lambda} \theta$$

$$s \cdot t \sum_{k=1}^{K} \lambda^{k,t} x_n^{k,t} \leq x_n^{k,t}, n = 1, \ldots \ldots N$$

$$\sum_{k=1}^{K} \lambda^{k,t} y_m^{k,t} \geq y_m^{k,t} / \theta, m = 1, \ldots \ldots M \tag{4}$$

$$\sum_{k=1}^{K} \lambda^{k,t} \leq 1$$

When restating equation (4) with the equation of the output-based technical efficiency analysis by Farrell, equation (5) is set up.

$$D_o^t(x^{k,t}, y^{k,t})^{-1} = \max_{\phi, \lambda} \phi$$

$$s \cdot t \quad -\theta y_{k,t} + \Upsilon_t \lambda \geq 0,$$

$$x_{k,t} - X_t \lambda \geq 0, \tag{5}$$

$$\lambda \geq 0$$

The remaining three distance functions are calculated in the same way.

$$D_o^{t+1}(x^{k,t+1}, y^{k,t+1})^{-1} = \max_{\phi,\lambda} \phi$$
$$s \cdot t \quad -\theta y_{k,t+1} + \Upsilon_{t+1}\lambda \geq 0,$$
$$x_{k,t+1} - X_{t+1}\lambda \geq 0,$$
$$\lambda \geq 0$$
\hfill (6)

$$D_o^{t}(x^{k,t+1}, y^{k,t+1})^{-1} = \max_{\phi,\lambda} \phi$$
$$s \cdot t \quad -\theta y_{k,t+1} + \Upsilon_t\lambda \geq 0,$$
$$x_{k,t+1} - X_t\lambda \geq 0,$$
$$\lambda \geq 0$$
\hfill (7)

$$D_o^{t+1}(x^{k,t}, y^{k,t})^{-1} = \max_{\phi,\lambda} \phi$$
$$s \cdot t \quad -\theta y_{k,t} + \Upsilon_{t+1}\lambda \geq 0,$$
$$x_{k,t} - X_{t+1}\lambda \geq 0,$$
$$\lambda \geq 0$$
\hfill (8)

In order to calculate the efficiency changes of 7 regional branches over 5 years using the distance function above, 28 equations need to be solved for the values of 4 linear programming. Also, as another period is added, the chained index is needed, so when there are n DMUs and the period t, the equation looks as follows: $n \times (3t - 2)$. In this research, DEAP version 2.1 (Data Envelopment Analysis computer program) is utilized to calculate the linear programming.

IV. Result

1. *Productivity change of Hansalim Seoul*

The basic statistics of panel data of Hansalim Seoul are shown in Table 7.4. The number of members applied reflects the increment in members of each relevant year only. The number of members participating in management and activities includes those participating in branch management meetings, local unit management meetings, member-based organizations, urban-rural inter-change and so on. The turnover ratio of reusable bottles is calculated comparing the number of bottles supplied to members with that returned to Hansalim Seoul. The farmland contribution area is calculated by dividing the cultivation area of the relevant year by that of the previous year based on the farmland area statistics sourcebook from the National Statistical Office. Each year's cultivation areas of Hansalim Seoul are classified into the rice paddy (20 pyong/

Table 7.4 Average and standard deviation valuable of inputs and outputs

			2012	2013	2014	2015	2016
Input	Members	Average	23,190	26,683	30,556	33,676	36,238
Input	Members	Standard deviation	3,366	4,243	4,756	4,735	4,850
Input	Participative members	Average	3,224	2,972	3,542	3,386	4,085
Input	Participative members	Standard deviation	1,127	643	985	964	1,015
Input	Labor cost (1,000 won)	Average	1,402,931	1,599,545	1,842,277	2,116,804	2,217,607
Input	Labor cost (1,000 won)	Standard deviation	115,861	127,198	213,927	222,791	212,002
Out-put	Reusable bottle collection rate (%)	Average	0.12	0.13	0.13	0.18	0.20
Out-put	Reusable bottle collection rate (%)	Standard deviation	0.02	0.01	0.01	0.03	0.02
Out-put	Farmland contribution area (%)	Average	0.0002	0.0002	0.0002	0.0002	0.0003
Out-put	Farmland contribution area (%)	Standard deviation	0.0000	0.0000	0.0000	0.0000	0.0000
Out-put	Sales (1,000 won)	Average	17,532,493	20,319,511	22,115,961	23,015,907	24,160,420
Out-put	Sales (1,000 won)	Standard deviation	4,000,112	4,860,954	5,613,591	5,497,617	5,281,232

Table 7.5 Malmquist productivity index and components change rates

Periods	TFP	TECI	TCI	PECI	SECI
2012/2013	1.013	0.986	1.027	1.000	0.986
2013/2014	0.932	0.997	0.935	0.990	1.008
2014/2015	1.072	0.987	1.086	1.000	0.987
2015/2016	1.010	1.034	0.997	1.011	1.023
Mean	1.006	1.001	1.005	1.000	1.001

Note: $\ln M = \ln E + \ln T$

person), the fruits (4.3 pyong/person), greenhouse crops (1.9 pyong/person), outdoor cultivation (9.0 pyong/person) – note that *pyong* is a land measure of six chucks (≒1.8 mm square).

The result of the analysis of productivity change and the rates of change of the components from 2012 to 2016 are shown in Table 7.5. The annual average productivity of Hansalim Seoul measured for five years from 2012 to 2016 increased by 0.6%; 1.3% in 2012/2013, 7.2% in 2014/2015, 1.0% in 2015/2016 increased, whereas the productivity from 2013 to 2014 decreased by 6.8% (Table 7.5).

Over 2014 and 2015 when the productivity raised the most by 7.2%, it was TCI that exerted a direct influence on the productivity index change, which showed a rise of 8.6%. The technical change here refers to a higher possibility of producing more outputs with the same level of inputs when production change is extended. With the same input, the case where the increase in output is more likely to happen is called *technical advance* and the opposite case is defined as *technical regression* (Lee and Oh, 2012). A technical advance is a concept that embraces changes of organizational regulation or organization culture, which can be seen as a turning point of the biographical and structural paradigm of the organization system (Yoo, 2005). Therefore, the reasons why TCI during this period has increased may be explained by searching what Hansalim Seoul and each branch have tried over the same period. The remarkable changes in this period are a reorganization of local organizations and policy support in relation to the collection of reusable bottles.

The years 2014 and 2015 were a period when a local organization for each regional branch was formed based on an administration unit in order to encourage more active members' participation. The local organizations of Hansalim Seoul focus on 'local' and 'basic organization' activities and play a role as a geographical base for members in regional areas to train self-governance (or autonomy) through various activities. Hansalim Seoul held a 'conference for local organization policy' for each regional branch in 2014 and established five local organizations with members' voluntary participation in 2014 and 2015, and also three local organizations in 2016. As of 2016, they currently have eight local organizations.

In terms of the reusable bottle collection promoted politically by Hansalim Seoul and the regional branches, there was a wide range of efforts. Firstly, they chose a way to constantly expose environment-related issues to their members by creating badges for promotion and distributing them to places members and supply executives use the most. Secondly, the label on bottles was supplemented with easily removable film so that members could find it convenient to remove the label when returning the bottle to the store. Thirdly, members had opportunities to visit the factory of reusable bottles and monitor the process of how those bottles are reused, understanding the collection policy. Another method was to implement the policy that they would receive a corresponding amount of equity when members return the reusable bottles they bought. Stores run by the regional branches also carried out more than 100 relevant events. Such efforts seem to have consequently led to over 20% of the collection rates.

On the other hand, the cause of the decrease of the technical efficiency by 1.3% during the same period is the decrease of the scale efficiency. It is assumed that the factor, which has influenced the fall of the scale efficiency, is related to stores of Hansalim Seoul that were newly opened. The number of stores that were established between 2014 and 2015 was 13, which is a large number compared to that of other periods. There are two problems caused by opening new stores, the increase in fixed costs and low growth basis, which are understood as influential to the scale efficiency. Fixed costs, generally, rise inevitably when opening up and running a new store because there needs to be expense such as rental fees, cost for equipment, labor cost and so on, whereas it takes a long time for the store to have gained after the break-even point, which generates a gap between time and expense. It is a very demanding job for the new store to be run at an optimal scale or to reach the break-even point in a short time. Thus, it is suggested that a specific strategy and tactics should be prepared for establishing new stores with consideration for sales that rise every year and expense that occurs when opening the stores.

2. *Productivity changes of regional branches of Hansalim Seoul*

In the productivity changes of seven regional branches of Hansalim Seoul, five branches showed the overall improvement in productivity from 2012 to 2016 and two experienced the productivity decrease (Table 7.6). Especially the first, third and fifth branches had productivity rises of 1.8%, 1.8% and 1.6%, respectively, and technical change index (TCI), which has the greatest impact on them, grew by 1.8%, 1.8% and 0.9% each. For branches 1, 3 and 5, the percentage of labor cost and the rate of increase in members who participate in management and activities are similar to those of other branches, while the number of those actively involved in management and activities seemed to have increased every year or maintained a similar number as the previous year. Likewise, branch 2 showed the productivity increase of 1.1%, which is relatively smaller than the

Table 7.6 Rate of change of Malmquist productivity index and components for each branch

Branch	TFP	TECI	TCI	PECI	SECI
1	1.018	1.000	1.018	1.000	1.000
2	1.011	1.000	1.011	1.000	1.000
3	1.018	1.000	1.018	1.000	1.000
4	1.002	1.000	1.002	1.000	1.000
5	1.016	1.007	1.009	1.000	1.007
6	0.982	1.000	0.982	1.000	1.000
7	0.993	1.000	0.993	1.000	1.000
Mean	1.006	1.001	1.005	1.000	1.001

Note: $\ln M = \ln E + \ln T$

increase rates of the three branches mentioned above. It is because the labor cost of branch 2 was estimated higher than that of the other branches, despite constant the members' participation in different campaigns and activities. In terms of branches 6 and 7, the productivity rates of which have decreased by 1.8% and 0.7% each, TCI is thought of as having affected the decrease in productivity. To put it another way, these two branches have experienced technical regression. In 2015 and 2016, fewer members were involved in management and activities than the previous year and the overall number of active members is relatively small, according to the base data of branches 6 and 7. When other inputs except the member participation are not significantly different to those of other branches, therefore, it is assumed that the decrease of the member participation is the main reason of the drop of the productivity.

V. Conclusion

Cooperative is defined as 'inferior organizations' by Alchian and Demsetz (1972), Furubotn (1976) and Jensen and Meckling (1979), who reviewed the principle of cooperative management. Such an evaluation is based on the frame of monitoring, horizon problem, common property, and non-transferability and control problem. What can be obtained from their assertion is that there is a difference between how firms are governed and how cooperatives are managed. It is implausible to explain this difference practically within the frame of the mainstream theories.

Similarly, there are Porter and Scully (1987) and Ferrier and Porter (1991), who have conducted research on cooperatives from the efficiency perspective. They argue that it is inevitable for cooperatives to have high management costs due to their values, which leads to the regression of technical efficiency. According to them, furthermore, allocative efficiency of cooperatives would be at a low level as they have a narrow spectrum of investment. Their argument is also regarded as having resulted from comparing performances of two types of firms that have different managing structure and aims using the identical standard of evaluation.

In contrast, Bontems and Fulton (2005) point out the advantages of cooperative management such as being able to compromise their aims in reflecting their members' intentions and sharing information based on altruism. There is another positive argument about cooperative management that cooperatives could generate better management efficiency under the economic condition of low profits because of low agency cost (Hueth and Marcoul, 2007).

The arguments that cooperatives are an inferior organizational structure have in common that they examine whether the organizational structure of general firms or that of cooperatives outweighs the other based on the firm theories. When analyzing firms like cooperatives that generate social benefits, however, it is inappropriate to compare them with general firms applying the firm theories only. This study argues values and unconventional performance of firms should be scrutinized in a way that is suitable for their ultimate purpose and management principle.

Thus, the present research has attempted to see what effects the values of cooperatives such as member participation as an association possessing the characteristics and orientation of both an economic organization and an association have on the performance. In relation to the research aim, the researchers have applied varying indicators to analyze the performance of cooperatives as well as financial indicators that are only capable of confirming the current status of the firm through financial ratios from several dimensions (e.g. sales, liquidity, solvency, etc.). As a result of the analysis of the productivity change Hansalim Seoul has experienced, the productivity of cooperatives can be different from that is examined. And the performance can be explained by the ways in which social benefits are included in the performance or not. The main interpretation of the productivity change of the seven regional branches is as follows.

From 2012 to 2016, in which the research was conducted, the productivity of Hansalim Seoul increased by 0.6, which is the annual average. In the case of 2014/2015 when the productivity rose by 7.2%, the most influential factor is a technical change, which has resulted from the reorganization establishing local organizations and the political support to encourage member participation into the reusable bottle collecting campaign.

That the reorganization of Hansalim Seoul has affected the productivity change corresponds with the argument by Putnam et al. (1994) that there appear to be cooperative behaviors with which members can agree through diverse activities and the accumulated behaviors lead to organizational efficiency and social efficiency, referring to the optimal distribution of resources in society. In addition, it is noteworthy that Hansalim Seoul took its members to the reusable bottle cleaning factory so as to share the aims of their activities, the movement and the campaigns. They also enabled those who return the reusable bottle they purchased to earn the corresponding amount of equity. As shown in Mutual Incentive theory by Birchall and Simmons (2004), it is vital to creating values that are sharable and a sense of community for members in order to prompt member's cooperation and participation. When providing acceptable rewards for the cooperative behaviors is meaningful, the efforts Hansalim Seoul made suggest what activities should be accompanied to stimulate member participation.

Concerning the productivity change of each branch, five out of seven branches showed the general improvement in productivity, whereas the others experienced the regression. The three branches with increased productivity, especially, were seen as influenced by technical change (TEC) the most. Based on the data used for the analysis, the number of members who participate in governance and activities in those branches has constantly increased every year, or showed the similar level to the previous year, compared to other branches. In contrast, the two branches with decreased productivity showed the lower rates of activities in which members participate in 2015 and 2016 and the number of those participating in governance and activities is relatively small. When the other inputs are not significantly different, the productivity regression of these two branches seems to have resulted from the declined number of participating members.

It is member participation in management and activities that have affected the productivity change of Hansalim Seoul. In order to encourage that, it is important to make members informed about shared values and shared goals of the cooperative and provide a means for them to engage in activities through pertinent policies.

The precedent studies reviewed have been on efficiency and productivity of the credit, agricultural, fisheries and dairy cooperatives, but not consumer cooperatives. Therefore, the present study that examines the effects cooperative member participation has on productivity change is significant in terms of having provided a way of analyzing cooperative, which is a dual-purpose organization and having formalized the requirements for effective management of cooperatives.

This research has been conducted so as to figure out the influence of member participation on productivity change in cooperatives. However, only Hansalim Seoul was dealt with can be said a limitation of this research. The reason was to ensure the homogeneity of decision-making units. To apply the Malmquist productivity index, it is necessary to secure the homogeneity of decision-making units but other local cooperatives in Hansalim association and Hansalim Seoul showed the difference in their scale. Comparing with other consumer cooperatives was unavailable as each cooperative has a different management style and there was difficulty in selecting the common non-financial indicators when considering inputs and outputs. Having said that, taking only Hansalim Seoul into account is a flaw to be supplemented.

Although Hansalim Seoul has organized and promoted various activities acknowledging that member participation is crucial in management ever since it was established, the systematization of archiving data relevant to member participation of individual branches was executed since 2014. Before the systematization, the general assembly sourcebook every year has done the job giving information about the way in which members engage in activities and the status of member participation. However, there was no identical way of resource archiving shared by all branches, which leads to difficulty in securing the homogeneity and measuring long-term productivity change. In other words, using resources and data only that were homogenous and usable can be seen as another limitation of this research. Despite such a restriction, however, it has been proved that member participation and policies are the most essential elements in cooperatives.

Research findings show that the changes in cooperative policies have affected the change of productivity to the greatest extent. It is assumed that further studies on influences of policy changes in consumer cooperatives on their performance could be conducted in the future. Furthermore, the policy subdividing the regional branches into local organizations that effectively encouraged member participation could lead to empirical analyses of to what extent the scale of cooperative should be enlarged for the best outcome. As the scale of consumer cooperatives expands and there are increasing concerns that member participation in management and activities becomes superficial, research on the meaningful relationship between the scale of organization and member participation would be useful when consumer cooperatives establish policies dividing and integrating their organizations.

References

Alchian, A. A., and Demsetz, H. (1972) 'Production, Information Costs, and Economic Organization.' *The American Economic Review*, 62(5): 777–795.

Argandona, A. (1998) 'The Stakeholder Theory and the Common Good.' *Journal of Business Ethics*, 17(9–10): 1093–1102.

Banker, R. D., Charnes, A., and Cooper, W. W. (1984) 'Some Models for Estimating Technical and Scale Inefficiencies in Data Envelopment Analysis.' *Management Science*, 30(9): 1078–1092.

Barros, C. P., and Santos, J. G. (2007) 'Comparing the Productive Efficiency of Cooperatives and Private Enterprises: The Portuguese Wine Industry as a Case Study.' *Journal of Rural Cooperation*, 35(2): 109–130.

Birchall, J., and Simmons, R. (2004) 'What Motivates Members to Participate in Cooperative and Mutual Businesses.' *Annals of Public and Cooperative*, 75(3): 465–495.

Bontems, P., and Fulton, M. (2005) 'Organizational Structure and the Endogeneity of Cost: Cooperatives, For-Profit Firms and the Cost Procurement.' *Institute National De La Recherche Agronomique-Unite d'Economie et Sociologie Rurales*, 310–339.

Charnes, A., Cooper, W. W., and Rhodes, E. (1978) 'Measuring the Efficiency of Decision Making Units.' *European Journal of Operational Research*, 2(6): 429–444.

Choi, J. Y., Nam, S. H., and Kang, S. K. (2003) 'Hanguk susanyeop hyeopdongjo-hapui kyeongyeong hyoyulsyeng pyeongga: galyopolak bunseok' [Evaluating Managerial Efficiency of Fisheries Cooperatives in Korea: Data Envelopment Analysis]. *The Journal of Fisheries Administration*, 34(2): 109–129.

Coase, R. H. (1937) 'The Nature of the Firm.' *Economica*, 4(16): 386–405.

Färe, R., Grosskopf, S., Lindgren, B., and Roos, P. (1994) 'Productivity Developments in Swedish Hospitals: A Malmquist Output Index Approach.' In Charnes, A., Cooper, W. W., Lewin, A. Y., and Seiford, L. M. (eds.), *Data Envelopment Analysis: Theory, Methodology, and Applications*. Berlin: Springer Science & Business Media, pp. 253–272.

Färe, R., Grosskopf, S., Norris, M., and Zhang, Z. (1994) 'Productivity Growth Technical Progress, and Efficiency Change in Industrialized Countries.' *The American Economic Review*, 84(1): 66–83.

Farrell, M. J. (1957) 'The Measurement of Productive Efficiency.' *Journal of the Royal Statistical Society*, 120(3): 253–290.

Ferrier, G. D. (1994) 'Ownership Type, Property Rights, and Relative Efficiency', in Charnes, A., Cooper, W. W., Lewin, A. Y., and Seiford, L. M. (eds.), *Data Envelopment Analysis: Theory, Methodology, and Applications*. Berlin: Springer Science & Business Media, pp. 273–283.

Ferrier, G. D., and Porter, P. K. (1991) 'The Productivity Efficiency of US Milk Processing Cooperatives.' *Journal of Agricultural Economics*, 42(2): 161–173.

Foss, N. J. (1993) 'Theories of the Firm: Contractual and Competence Perspectives.' *Journal of Evolutionary Economics*, 3(2): 127–144.

Furubotn, E. G. (1976) 'The Long-Run Analysis of the Labor-Managed Firm: An Alternative Interpretation.' *The American Economic Review*, 66(1): 104–123.

Grossman, S. J., and Hart, O. D. (1986) 'The Costs and Benefits of Ownership: A Theory of Vertical and Lateral Integration.' *The Journal of Political Economy*, 94(4): 691–719.

Guzman, I., and Arcas, N. (2008) 'The Usefulness of Accounting Information in the Measurement of Technical Efficiency in Agricultural Cooperatives.' *Annals of Public and Cooperative Economics*, 79(1): 107–131.

Hamel, G., and Prahalad, C. K. (1990) 'Corporate Imagination and Expeditionary Marketing.' *Harvard Business Review*, 69(4): 81–92.

Hart, O. (2011) 'Thinking about the Firm: A Review of Daniel Spulber's the Theory of the Firm.' *Journal of Economic Literature*, 49(1): 101–113.

Hodgson, G. M. (1998a) 'The Approach of Institutional Economics.' *Journal of Economic Literature*, 36(1): 166–192.

Hodgson, G. M. (1998b) 'Competence and Contract in the Theory of the Firm.' *Journal of Economic Behavior and Organization*, 35(2): 179–201.

Hong, B. Y., and Koo, C. O. (2000) 'DEAleul iyonghan sinyonghyeopdongjohapui hyoyulseong pyeongga' [A Data Envelopment Analysis of the Efficiency of Credit Unions]. *The Korean Journal of Financial Management*, 17(2): 277–292.

Hong, B. Y., Koo, C. O., and Choi, S. E. (2002) 'Sinyonghyeopdongjohapui saengsanseong byeonhwa cheukjeong' [Measurement of Change of Productivity of Credit Unions: 1997–2001]. *Korean Journal of Money & Finance*, 7(2): 93–111.

Hueth, B., and Marcoul, P. (2007) 'The Cooperative Firm as Monitored Credit,' Staff Paper No. 508, Madison, WI: Department of Agricultural & Applied Economics, University of Wisconsin-Madison.

Jang, D. H. (2011) 'Nonghyeop hanaromateuui DEA hyoyulseongwa Malmquist saengsanseong bunseok' [A DEA Efficiency and Malmquist Productivity Analysis for Nonghyup Hanaro Mart]. *Journal of Industrial Economics and Business*, 24(2): 953–967.

Jensen, M. C., and Meckling, W. H. (1979) 'Theory of the Firm: Managerial Behavior, Agency Costs, and Ownership Structure.' In Brunner, K. (ed.), *Economics Social Institutions*. Berlin: Springer Netherlands, pp. 163–231.

Kim, M. J. (2014) 'DEA mohyeong gibanui ecohoyulseonggwa gyongjejeok seonggwaui yeongwanseong' [The Relationship Between DEA Model-Based Eco-Efficiency and Economic Performance]. *Journal of Environmental Policy*, 13(4): 3–49.

Kim, Y. J., Kim, S. W., and Kim, Y. K. (2016) 'Jogik yeoklyang mich hyeopeob feuroseseuga kieupunyeongseongkwae michineun yeonghyange gwanhan yeongu' [A Study on the Effect of a Supplier's Organizational Capability and Collaboration Process on Supply Chain Quality Performance: An Empirical Approach Based on the Experience of Small and Medium Enterprises in Korea]. *Journal of the Korean Production and Operations Management Society*, 27(2): 225–248.

Knight, F. H. (1921) *Risk, Uncertainty and Profit*. Eastford, CT: Martino Fine Books.

Kruse, D. L. (1993) *Profit Sharing: Does It Make a Difference*. Kalamazoo, MI: Upjohn Institute for Employment Research.

Lee, J. D., and Oh, D. H. (2012) *Hyoyulseong bunseokilon* [Theory of Efficiency Analysis: Data Envelopment Analysis]. Seoul, Korea: Jiphil Media.

Oh, H. J. (2010) 'DEA mohyeonge uihan susanyeophyeopdongjohapui kyeongyeonghyoyulsyeng cheukjeonge gwanhan yeongu' [A Study on the Management Efficiency of Fisheries Cooperatives by Data Envelopment Analysis]. *Journal of Industrial Economics and Business*, 23(2): 1077–1094.

Park, S. S., Lee, M. H., and Lee, J. K. (2015) 'Hyeopdongjohapgwa gonggeupsaseul hyeoplyeok' [Co-operatives and Supply Chain Collaboration]. *Journal of the Korean Production and Operations Management Society*, 26(3): 351–374.

Penrose, E. T. (1959) *The Theory of the Growth of the Firm*. Oxford: Oxford University Press.

Porter, P. K., and Scully, G. W. (1987) 'Economic Efficiency in Cooperatives.' *The Journal of Law and Economics*, 30(2): 489–512.

Posadas, R. C., and Cabanda, E. (2011) 'Assessing Productivity Performance of Regional Electric Cooperatives in the Philippines.' *International Business & Economics Research Journal*, 6(8): 73.

Putnam, R. D., Leonard, R., and Nanetti, R. Y. (1994) *Making Democracy Work: Civic Traditions in Modern Italy*. Princeton, NJ: Princeton University Press.

Selznick, P. (1997) *Leadership in Administration: A Sociological Interpretation: Resources Firms and Strategies*. Oxford: Oxford University Press.

Thompson, S. P. (2015a) *Bringing Society Back into the Theory of the Firm: The Adaptation of the Mondragon Cooperative Model in Valencia and Beyond*. Doctoral Dissertation, Centre of Development Studies. Cambridge: University of Cambridge.

Thompson, S. P. (2015b) 'Towards a Social Theory of the Firm: Worker Cooperatives Reconsidered.' *Journal of Co-operative Organization and Management*, 3(1): 3–13.

Valentinov, V. L. (2004) 'Toward a Social Capital Theory of Cooperative Organization.' *Journal of Cooperative Studies*, 37(3): 5–20.

Veblen, T. (1908) 'On the Nature of Capital.' *The Quarterly Journal of Economics*, 22(4): 517–542.

Williamson, O. E. (1975) *Markets and Hierarchies: Analysis and Antitrust Implications: A Study in the Economics of Internal Organization*. Champaign, IL: University of Illinois at Urbana-Champaign's Academy for Entrepreneurial Leadership Historical Research Reference in Entrepreneurship.

Winter, S. G. (1988) 'On Coase, Competence, and the Corporation.' *Journal of Law, Economics and Organization*, 4(1): 163–180.

Yoo, K. R. (2002) 'Oehwanwigi iwho jibangsangsudosayeopui saengsanseong byeonhwa bunseok' [An Empirical Analysis of the Productivity Change of Korean Water Supply Services After the Financial Crisis]. *Korean Public Administration Review*, 36(4): 281–301.

Yoo, K. R. (2005) 'Gonggongbumunui saengsanseong cheukjeongeul wihan bibangsajeok mamquist saengsanseong jisuui cheukjeong bangbeobgwa jeokyong' [Measurement Methods and Their Application of the Non-Radical Malmquist Productivity Index for Measuring the Productivity of the Public Sector]. *International Journal of Policy Evaluation & Management*, 15(2): 99–125.

8 Consumer cooperatives and supply chain management

Dasom Kim, Sangsun Park and Seungkwon Jang

I. Introduction

This chapter focuses on the 'collaborative supply chain management (SCM)' of consumer cooperatives. With several factors explored by empirical and theoretical investigations, a causal loop diagram shows a basic principle of collaborative SCM in Korea's consumer cooperative, iCOOP. As we aim to understand the basic principle of cooperation among ultimate consumers and suppliers, we do not include every single supply chain entity of the supply chain. Thus, we draw a causal loop diagram, which leads to system dynamics (SD) simulation. The chapter is conceptual exploration, not practical and quantitative research.

Customers, manufacturers, retailers, and suppliers have realized they have to cooperate with other entities for mutually beneficial reasons based on value exchange relationship in order to survive in the market of cut-throat competition (Sahay, 2003). This trend of SCM makes individual business entities extend their organizational boundaries and pursue a collaborative relationship with other business entities rather than seeking their own benefits only. A supply chain can be extended to as far as organization's ultimate suppliers and ultimate consumers, creating an 'ultimate supply chain' (Mentzer et al., 2001).

The purpose of SCM research is to examine the best practice that enhances supply chain performance (Lee, 2009). However, there is no research that has examined consumer cooperative cases of collaborative SCM including ultimate suppliers and consumers. It is necessary to explore the best practice of the collaborative and ultimate SCM.

In order to discuss a case of collaborative and ultimate SCM, we decided to investigate consumer cooperatives, which have involved ultimate consumers in its supply chain. Especially, most Korean consumer cooperatives have close relationships with ultimate suppliers as their supply chain partners. Thus, we have studied a case of iCOOP, due to its supply chain within which ultimate suppliers and ultimate consumers participate. While investigating iCOOP's business practices, it is possible to gain knowledge about how to manage a collaborative supply chain sustainably when it includes ultimate suppliers and ultimate consumers.

In this chapter, we aim to figure out the basic management principle that encourages multi-stakeholders, especially consumers and suppliers, to collaborate in a supply chain enhancing the whole supply chain performance sustainably. For this purpose, we have employed SD methodology, which enables an examination of long-term sustainability of SCM. Since we were unable to complete the simulation yet, only until the causal loop diagram is presented in this research.

II.   System dynamics methodology

SD is chosen as a methodology to investigate iCOOP's collaborative SCM practice because it allows us to frame, understand, and discuss complex issues and problems with mathematical modeling. SD, invented by professor Jay Forrester of the Massachusetts Institute of Technology (MIT), has been used as an excellent tool to understand and improve corporate managerial processes, analyze and design policies, forecast and solve possible problems, and so on (Forrester, 1961).

The central concept of SD is 'interactive system'. It tries to understand how objects in a system interact with one another and also with the system. SD breaks up the world into smaller 'feedback loops', and observes dynamic behavior of the system with a holistic view. Based on such an understanding, we can build a computer model of the complex world and simulate long-term behavior of this dynamic interactive system.

The characteristics of SD could be explained as follows:

1   SD focuses on how dynamically the behavior of variables change over time (Meadows et al., 1972). Due to the dynamics of the system, the relative importance of the elements changes over time. Moreover, SD recognizes the effect of time lag.
2   SD sees that system elements show dynamic feedback response according to their circular causality (Meadows et al., 1972). It means no cause-and-effect relationships are in a linear relationship; all are in circular relationships.
3   A system embraces all the elements that cause dynamic changes in the research object.
4   SD is based on operational thinking. It focuses on how things really work, not how things are correlated with each other. Thus, it helps us understand the actual process of how things happen.

III.   iCOOP's business model and strategy

This research is primarily conducted on the basis of qualitative empirical research methods including various in-depth interviews of iCOOP managers and participant observations in iCOOP's head office and shops during the time between April 2011 and December 2011.[1] iCOOP's annual reports and other unpublished documents are also investigated. Through such investigations, we are able to highlight some noticeable features of iCOOP as a retail business.

1. iCOOP's business model

There are four features in iCOOP's business model. Firstly, as a Korea's consumer cooperative, iCOOP basically deals in organic agri-food product. Secondly, according to the Consumer Cooperative Law in Korea, the use of consumer cooperatives is restricted only to their members in principle.[2] For this reason, consumers should join in as a member in order to use iCOOP's business properly. Thirdly, like many Korea's consumer cooperative associations, iCOOP has many suppliers as their supply chain partners. iCOOP does not deal with suppliers who have not contracted with them as their partner or as their temporary supplier. Fourthly, iCOOP has a highly integrated distribution system. They can share information on demand, supply and production with both suppliers and consumers.

Considering its business model, iCOOP has a good environment for collaborative SCM. Although they are not managing their supply chain as ideal 'ultimate supply chain', they are very close to it. The research scope of this chapter is only considering consumer members and partner suppliers in iCOOP's supply chain, in which the basic management principle maintains the cooperation between multi-stakeholders, including consumers and suppliers in a supply chain.

2. iCOOP's strategy

iCOOP has been very successful in its business since its establishment in 1997.[3] It has achieved excellent performance through collaboration among consumer members and partner suppliers. Compared to other consumer cooperatives in Korea, iCOOP has several unique strategies. The most successfully implementing strategy is to introduce the system of the 'membership due'.

iCOOP has started the membership due ever since its establishment. It is a strategy that consumer members pay the monthly dues to their local cooperative, about $10 per month, while they shop at a discounted price. The discounted price for members is almost the same as the wholesale price, which is about 20% cheaper on average than non-member's price.

Membership dues are different from member's equity. It is non-refundable to consumers so that it provides more stable capital to iCOOP and its local primary cooperatives. A total of 50% of the dues are used for improving consumer services, cover operational costs and so on. The other half has been appropriated by primary cooperatives in order to support its local activities. With membership dues, consumer members are contributing to their local cooperative and iCOOP's business thus supporting partner suppliers consequently. Moreover, by increasing asset specificity, membership dues improve consumer member's loyalty to cooperative. iCOOP has reported membership-due-members have purchased much more goods and services from iCOOP than non-membership-due-members.[4] It gave iCOOP a reason to require obligatory membership due payment to its consumer members. Furthermore, a fixed amount[5] of equity payment is required on each purchase. It increases asset specificity, the loyalty of consumer members, and strengthens iCOOP's finance.

With consumer members having high loyalty, iCOOP can predict consumer's needs and changes of seasonal demand more easily. And they can implement various management policies, which require consumer members' collaboration. In this regard, the strategy of membership dues plays a crucial role in iCOOP's collaborative SCM.

IV.   Supply chain management (SCM)

1.   *Theories of supply chain management*

As Mentzer et al. (2001) suggest an integrated frame of SCM both practically and academically, the characteristics of SCM philosophy are as follows:

1   A systems approach to viewing the supply chain as a whole and to managing the total flow of goods inventory from the supplier to the ultimate customer
2   A strategic orientation towards cooperative efforts to synchronize and converge intra-firm and inter-firm operational and strategic capabilities into a unified whole
3   A customer focus to create unique and individualized sources of customer value, leading to customer satisfaction.

When studying SCM, the macro level of results that individual entities in a supply chain generated at a micro level must be included, and it must be focused on cooperative activities of the entire entities in a supply chain. Although there are various definitions of supply chain, we adopted the definition from Mentzer et al. (2001: 4):

> Supply chain is defined as a set of three or more entities (organizations or individuals) directly involved in the upstream and downstream flows of products, services, finances, and/or information from a source to a customer.

Such a supply chain can be identified into three degrees by its complexity (Mentzer et al., 2001): a direct supply chain, an extended supply chain and an ultimate supply chain. No matter how complex the supply chain is, it exists as a phenomenon and the final consumer is always considered as a member of a supply chain (Mentzer et al., 2001). From various definitions of SCM, Mentzer et al. (2001: 18) extracted the definition of SCM:

> Supply chain management is defined as the systemic, strategic coordination of the traditional business functions and the tactics across these business functions within a particular company and across businesses within the supply chain, for the purposes of improving the long-term performance of the individual companies and the supply chain as a whole.

2.   Recent development of supply chain management

At first, the traditional view of SCM was based on arms-length negotiations, partner evaluation depending on purchase price, cost-based information, multiple partners and so on to achieve the lowest initial purchase prices while ensuring supply (Spekman et al., 1998; Matthyssens and Van den Bulte, 1994; Sahay, 2003). Due to the dynamics of the supply chain such as bullwhip effect, however, co-operation among supply chain entities (i.e. information sharing) became an important issue in SCM. Bullwhip effect was named by Lee et al. (1997), but first found by Forrester (1961). Forrester (1961) found that demand information is amplified and distorted while passing supply chain entities from downstream to upstream. Ironically, it is caused by supply chain players' rational behavior. Because of the lack of information sharing between buyers and sellers, the bullwhip effect is inevitable and, consequently, incurs a huge amount of cost in the whole supply chain. Lee et al. (1997) argue that, in order to eliminate the bullwhip effect, not decision makers' behavior but the structure of the supply chain and its related processes should be modified. Recently, supply chain entities including customers, manufactures, retailers and suppliers have realized that they have to come together for mutually beneficial reasons based on value exchange relationship in order to survive in the market (Sahay, 2003).

The basic principle of SCM is win-win cooperation (Lee and Shin, 2008), which is formed with the expectation of mutual benefit among independent organizations. Moreover, modern manufacturing philosophies have forced evolution of relationships between buyers and suppliers (Maloni and Benton, 1997). Through the partnership, supply chain entities can expect a synergetic supply chain in which the entire chain is more effective than the sum of its individual parts (Maloni and Benton, 1997). As a result, end consumer will hopefully receive higher quality and cost-effective products or services (Maloni and Benton, 1997). Also, Lee (2009) suggested that collaborative SCM is not an altruistic behavior. Rather, we have to realize that it brings a positive boomerang effect of capability.

The trend of collaboration in supply chain generates people's concern on the right way of collaboration to enhance the performance of the whole supply chain (Huang et al., 2003; Simchi-Levi et al., 2004; Zhang, 2007). Shin et al. (2000) argue that it is essential to form a close relationship between buyers and suppliers in order to manage a collaborative supply chain effectively. The 'close relationship' in this context means a willingness to share risks and rewards and maintain the relationship with partners over a long period of time (Chen and Paulraj, 2004).

The close relationship among partners is directly related to trust. For example, information sharing among partners reduces the uncertainty of a partner's behavior and thus enhances trust between partners. Consequently, it leads to the improvement of the whole supply chain performance by raising the commitment of partners to each other (Kwon and Suh, 2004; Kwon and Suh, 2005). Therefore, in the next section, we will explore the role of trust in the buyer-supplier relationship.

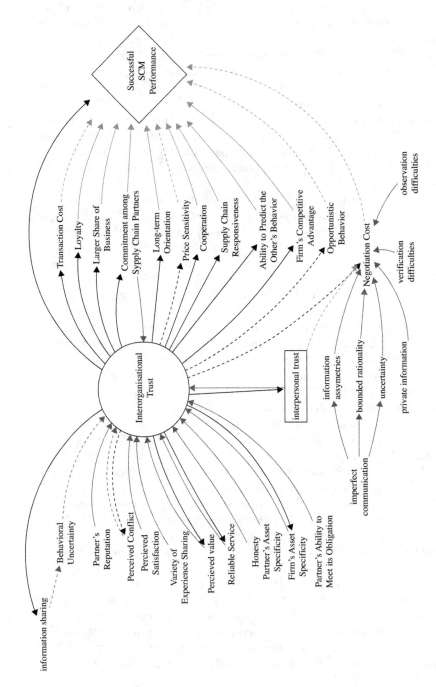

Figure 8.1 The relationships between trust and SCM performance

Note: a solid line (—) indicates a positive relationship, a dotted line (- - -) indicates a negative relationship.

3.   The role of trust in buyer-supplier relationships

Among many determinants of cooperation, Smith et al. (1995) found that trust is the most important and immediate antecedent of cooperation. Sahay (2003) also emphasized that trust plays a very significant role in a supply chain partnership. What is trust then? Doney and Cannon (1997: 36) define trust as 'perceived credibility and benevolence of a target of trust'. It refers that 'a buying firm facing some degree of risk in a purchase situation turns to a supplier or salesperson that the buyer believes is able to perform effectively and reliably (credible) and is interested in the customer's best interests (benevolent)' (Doney and Cannon, 1997: 36).

There are many studies about the role of trust as well as the factors that draw trust for successful SCM (Handfield and Bechtel, 2002; Kwon and Suh, 2004; Kwon and Suh, 2005; Lui, Wong and Liu, 2008; Narayandas and Rangan, 2004; Sahay, 2003; Smith and Barclay, 1997; Smith et al., 1995; Welty and Becerra-Fernandez, 2001; Zaheer et al., 1998). We integrate the result of these studies in Figure 8.1. We point out the factors that invoke trust on the left side of the 'interorganisational trust', and the results of trust on the right side of 'interorganisational trust'. The results of trust can be seen as supply chain performance.

V.   Causal loop diagram

The white boxes of Figure 8.2 are the factors that cause trust between supply chain entities. The black boxes are the results of trust in a supply chain. We can find that consumers' participation of membership dues creates both causes of trust and results of trust. In iCOOP's supply chain, the causes and the results of trust affect each other positively, so the consumers and suppliers in iCOOP can collaborate with each other based on trust (consumer transaction cost and asset specificity). For example, when seeing the bold arrows in Figure 8.2, we can notice two loops that influence each other. Firstly, we will have a look at the smaller loop. When a consumer joins in iCOOP as a member, the total number of membership dues participation rises. Paying membership dues increases consumers' asset specificity to iCOOP because members have to pay non-refundable membership dues every month. In order to offset the membership dues, members consume more groceries they need from iCOOP instead of going to other supermarket chains. However, iCOOP imposes the fixed amount of equity capital payment every time members make a purchase, which reinforces asset specificity of members. Increased asset specificity enhances members' loyalty to iCOOP. As consumers' loyalty increases, the number of membership withdrawal decreases. As a whole, these links make a positive feedback loop that strengthens and signals members' loyalty to iCOOP and suppliers as well.

Secondly, let's move on to the bigger loop. Increase in membership due members makes it easier for managers and suppliers to predict consumers' behavior, which in turn decreases suppliers' uncertainty about consumers' demand. As producers' uncertainty about consumers' demand decreases, producers' commitment to iCOOP increases. To put it another way, membership due members

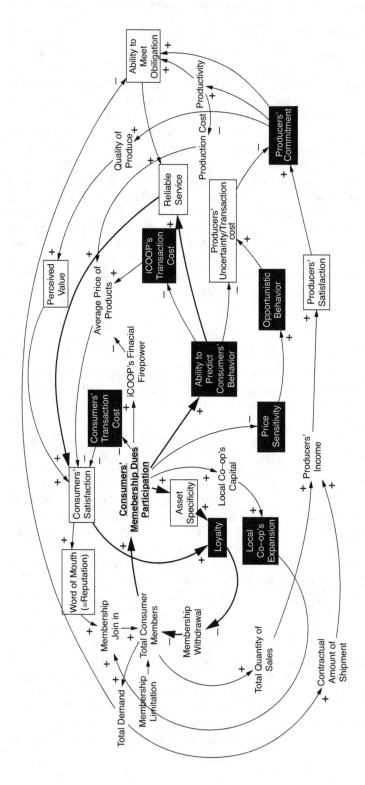

Figure 8.2 The causal loop diagram of iCOOP's SCM

Note: a link indicates interrelationship between two variables. A positive link (+) means that the linked variables change in the same direction. A negative link (−) indicates that the two nodes change in opposite directions.

enhance producers' commitment. It sequentially increases suppliers' ability to meet the demand of consumers, provide reliable services and fulfill consumers' satisfaction. It affects consumers' loyalty in turn.

In both two loops, it is noticeable that membership due participation generates the factors that result in trust. The initial factors that derived from membership due participation promote other factors of trust. It can be said that consumer's participation in membership due establishes positive feedback loops of trust and enhances the whole supply chain performance simultaneously.

VI.   Conclusion

In this chapter, we explored a collaborative SCM that includes ultimate suppliers and ultimate consumers. Based on the case study of iCOOP, the essential factors and strategies leading to the collaborative SCM include end-consumers and suppliers perform sustainably. As trust is the essential factor in a collaborative SCM, it is vital to building a business structure that systematically forms trust between supply chain partners, and that enhances the whole supply chain performance, so as to sustain the collaborative SCM. The structure of positive feedback loops will be constructed so that the system of the supply chain is continued.

We argue that it is possible to build a management structure that encourages co-operation among consumers and suppliers. From the case of iCOOP, we could point out there is no need of benevolent behavior of any particular supply chain entity when the organization can build trust in the whole supply chain through a good management structure.

The most distinguishing practice of iCOOP for the collaborative SCM is they have established a membership due strategy, which offers a stable consumer foothold. It helps a supply chain to be managed effectively. With the stable consumer member base, iCOOP can pursue various policies for collaborative SCM and can offer reliable income to suppliers with secured demand. Moreover, membership dues reduce consumers' opportunistic behavior and make them contribute to the supply chain. Lastly, because membership dues were not compulsory, participating in membership dues acted as a signal of consumers' trust in the cooperative and partner suppliers in the early days of iCOOP.

In conclusion, we can say that membership dues build trust in the supply chain of iCOOP and also enhances its supply chain performance. The comprehensive behavior of supply chain entities under a membership due system is a positive feedback model that makes it possible for all supply chain entities to cooperate with each other.

Notes

1 Since then, there were some changes in iCOOP's policy and its legal environment. Although it does not affect the core insights of this chapter, we have updated some noticeable changes and revised our causal loop diagram in Oct 2018.

2 There was a partial revision on the article 46, *use of business*, of the Law in March 2016. The amended law allows consumers' cooperatives to provide their business

services to non-members when it is specified by Ordinance of the Prime Minister for the smooth management of business services, such as advertisement or disposal of goods in stock. However, provision of services to non-members could be applied to limited circumstances. Thus, we could still say that use of consumer's cooperatives is restricted only to their members in principle.

3 The total number of iCOOP's consumer members in 2017 was 262,507 households with 55.5 billion won (approx. 48.6million dollar) of equity investments and 553.8 billion won (approx. 484.5million dollar) of sales. The details of iCOOP's business performance has been described in the Chapter 1.

4 Each consumer members have to purchase at least $50 per month in order to offset membership dues when we consider that membership-due-members get 20% discounts.

5 i.e. $0.5 on purchase between $5 to $20 and $1 on purchase over $20.

References

Chen, I. J., and Paulraj, A. (2004) 'Towards a Theory of Supply Chain Management: The Constructs and Measurements.' *Journal of Operations Management*, 22: 119–150.

Doney, P. M., and Cannon, J. P. (1997) 'An Examination of the Nature of Trust in Buyer-Seller Relationships.' *The Journal of Marketing*, 61(2): 35–51.

Forrester, J. W. (1961) *Industrial Dynamics*. Cambridge, MA: Massachusetts Institute of Technology Press.

Handfield, R. B., and Bechtel, C. (2002) 'The Role of Trust and Relationship Structure in Improving Supply Chain Responsiveness.' *Industrial Marketing Management*, 31: 367–382.

Huang, G., Lau, J., and Mak, K. L. (2003) 'The Impacts of Sharing Production Information on Supply Chain Dynamics: A Review of the Literature.' *International Journal of Production Research*, 41: 1483–1517.

Kwon, I. W. G., and Suh, T. (2004) 'Factors Affecting the Level of Trust and Commitment in Supply Chain Relationships.' *Journal of Supply Chain Management*, 40: 4–14.

Kwon, I. W. G., and Suh, T. (2005) 'Trust, Commitment and Relationships in Supply Chain Management: A Path Analysis.' *Supply Chain Management: An International Journal*, 10: 26–33.

Lee, H. L., Padmanabhan, V., and Whang, S. (1997) 'The Bullwhip Effect in Supply Chains.' *Sloan Management Review*, 38: 93–102.

Lee, S. Y. (2009) 'Hyupryukjuc gonggupsasil guanliga chamyeo giyup sungkwae michinun yonghyang-ae dehan yongu' [A Study on the Effects of Collaborative Supply Management Buyer and Supplier Performance: From a View of Capabilities Transfer Throughout the Supply Chain]. *Journal of the Korean Operations Research and Management Science Society*, 34: 85–104.

Lee, Y., and Shin, H. (2008) 'Gumei giyup-guae janggigeok goere guangei hyungsunghil wehan gonggup upchaei geonlak sooribe guanhan tamsekgeok yongu' [An Exploratory Study on the Suppliers' Strategy for Developing Long-Term Relationship With Buyers]. *Journal of the Korean Operations Research and Management Science Society*, 33: 13–30.

Lui, S. S., Wong, Y., and Liu, W. (2008) 'Asset Specificity Roles in Interfirm Cooperation: Reducing Opportunistic Behaviour or Increasing Cooperative Behaviour?' *Journal of Business Research*, 62(11): 1214–1219.

Maloni, M. J., and Benton, W. C. (1997) 'Supply Chain Partnerships: Opportunities for Operations Research.' *European Journal of Operational Research*, 101(3): 419–429.

Matthyssens, P., and Van den Bulte, C. (1994) 'Getting Closer and Nicer: Partnerships in the Supply Chain.' *Long Range Planning*, 27: 72–83.

Meadows, D. H., Meadows, D. H., Randers, J., and Behrens III, W. W. (1972) *The Limits to Growth: A Report to the Club of Rome*. Washington, DC: A Potomac Associates Book.

Mentzer, J. T., Keebler, W. J. S., Min, S., Nix, N. W., Smith, C. D., and Zacharia, Z. G. (2001) 'Defining Supply Chain Management.' *Journal of Business Logistics*, 22(2): 1–25.

Narayandas, D., and Rangan, V. K. (2004) 'Building and Sustaining Buyer-Seller Relationship in Mature Industrial Markets.' *Journal of Marketing*, 68(3): 63–77.

Sahay, B. S. (2003) 'Understanding Trust in Supply Chain Relationships.' *Industrial Management & Data Systems*, 103(8): 553–563.

Shin, H., Collier, D. A., and Wilson, D. D. (2000) 'Supply Management Orientation and Supplier/Buyer Performance.' *Journal of Operations Management*, 18(3): 317–333.

Simchi-Levi, D., Kaminsky, P., and Simchi-Levi, E. (2004) *Managing the Supply Chain: The Definitive Guide for the Business Professional*. New York, NY: McGraw-Hill Professional.

Smith, J. B., and Barclay, D. W. (1997) 'The Effects of Organizational Differences and Trust on the Effectiveness of Selling Partner Relationships.' *The Journal of Marketing*, 61(1): 3–21.

Smith, K. G., Carroll, S. J., and Ashford, S. J. (1995) 'Intra- and Interorganizational Cooperation: Toward a Research Agenda.' *The Academy of Management Journal*, 38(1): 7–23.

Spekman, R. E., Kamauff Jr., J. W., and Myhr, N. (1998) 'An Empirical Investigation into Supply Chain Management: A Perspective on Partnerships.' *Supply Chain Management: An International Journal*, 3(2): 53–67.

Welty, B., and Becerra-Fernandez, I. (2001) 'Managing Trust and Commitment in Collaborative Supply Chain Relationships.' *Communications of the ACM*, 44(6): 67–73.

Zaheer, A., McEvily, B., and Perrone, V. (1998) 'Does Trust Matter? Exploring the Effects of Interorganizational and Interpersonal Trust on Performance.' *Organization Science*, 9(2): 141–159.

Zhang, C. (2007) 'Design and Simulation of Demand Information Sharing in a Supply Chain.' *Simulation Modelling Practice and Theory*, 15(1): 32–46.

9 Conclusion

The future of Korea's consumer cooperatives

Seungkwon Jang, Ah Young Kim,
Bo Young Oh and Jihyun Jeong

Historically, social movement and civil society organizations have been the driving force of Korea's consumer cooperatives, which have been developing the social economy sector, or the third sector. Furthermore, consumer cooperatives have been able to be social innovators changing Korea's socio-economic structure and practices towards a balanced system. Big business groups, or *Chaebols*, have dominated Korea's economy since the 1960s when the industrialization had been planned and led by the state. Nevertheless, the last 20 years or so, Korea's consumer cooperatives are getting bigger and growing faster than other players along with the development of civil society. They have learned many successful factors from various sources, notably their own painstaking experiences and innovative experiments.

Based on the previous chapters, we can summarize the characteristics of Korea's consumer cooperatives as follows: (1) member-controlled (women members-dominated) governance, (2) direct selling business model of environmental-friendly agri-foods, (3) social movement and CSO (civil society organization), and social economy–oriented cooperative identity, (4) fast learning from their own experiences.

This book is about the past and present of Korea's consumer cooperatives. We have addressed, mainly, the present cooperative management practices such as governance and supply chain management. Thus, it allows readers to grasp the current dynamics of consumer cooperatives. In this concluding chapter, we argue how future cooperative challenges can be responded based on the Blueprint model (International Co-operative Alliance, 2013). Recently, major consumer cooperatives in Korea have been slowing down the growth of turnover and membership. In this regard, it is the right time to discuss the challenges and responses.

The Blueprint and Korea's consumer cooperatives

Since 1937, ICA has established seven principles to clarify the cooperative identity and value, which derived from the business success of the Rochdale Society of Equitable Pioneers in the 19th century (Fairbairn, 1994). Then the questions might be followed as such: What makes cooperatives establish the principles? And how cooperatives follow the principles? The answers reside in their fundamental dilemmas to satisfy social and economic needs which differ in time and place. Hence, it has been reviewed by researchers and practitioners how the distinctive features of cooperatives could contribute to their own competences (Fairbairn, 1994).

Cooperative seven principles have stated the definition and value of cooperatives referred to at the declaration of ICA General Assembly in Manchester, 1995. The seven principles have been revised continuously through the ICA General Assembly: Paris in 1937, Vienna in 1966 and lastly Manchester in 1995 (Fairbairn, 1994). The process of discussion and agreement indicates that the cooperative principles are not the fixed rules and indicators, but the reciprocal interpreting process of the significance of cooperatives in the dynamic social, historical, and economic context (Hilson, 2017). Therefore, the interpretation and guidelines of cooperative principles can vary with the incessant change of past, present, and future.

In addition to the principles, ICA has developed the Blueprint for Cooperative Decade (2013) to demonstrate that the cooperative business model is resilient and fast-growing enterprise model leading sustainable society, economy, and environment. It delivers the political and institutional legitimacy of cooperative identity by reinterpreting the seven principles against the dominance of a single business model – that is, an investor-owned company. Thus, they suggest an implementation strategy to achieve the 2020 vision based on five themes of the cooperative Blueprint. They mainly shed light on the cooperative identity in the Blueprint, which is supported by the other four themes – that is, participation, sustainability, legal framework, and capital. The themes of participation and sustainability differentiate the cooperatives from other enterprise models. Then, the legal framework and capital describe the conditions for the sustainability of cooperatives.

The first theme of the cooperative model is participation. The foremost feature that distinguishes the cooperative from other enterprise models would be the participation of member-owners in the decision-making process. The one-member-one-vote principle formally guarantees individual members' influences and participation in cooperative governance in two ways. Firstly, it realizes effective decision-making in the organization, thus offers a better way of doing business (International Co-operative Alliance, 2013: 4). Secondly, cooperatives play a central role as organizations to learn the skills to participate in the democratic decision-making process and engage in issues of communities and societies. In this regard, the Blueprint strategy aims to find out the best practices to enhance participation by providing member incentives and benefits. However, the significance of participation changes in the current socio-economic context. The global crisis and growing inequality prompt active participation. Besides, the emergence of digital and smart technologies problematizes the boundary of membership and accelerates the various forms of participation. Thus, it suggests we should explore the different levels of participation and membership beyond the existing member-user category and to prepare new strategies for interactive communication such as social and collaborative media. It would be interesting to see the challenges and opportunities with which Korean consumer cooperatives encounter.

Consumer cooperative has critically emphasized the importance of participation. Since democratic governance is not fully guaranteed by the one-member-one-vote principle, the practice of participation is significant for having its legitimacy. The governance practice of consumer cooperative based on the sensemaking process of communication is identified as generative governance which shifts the challenge to opportunity (see Chapter 2). This case study reveals the actual process of cooperative governance of member participation and necessitates the decision-making competency to improve their proficiency in management. In addition, the analyses of Hansalim Seoul provide that the member controls and participation of consumer cooperatives contribute to productivity increase (see Chapter 7). The cooperative's shared values and goals help engage members in cooperative businesses.

However, low participation of young people remains a challenge for consumer cooperatives in Korea. It goes along with the sustainability of the cooperative model in the future. In the era of knowledge economy and network society, especially with the help of the Internet, there seem to be a rapid and increasing needs of citizens to solve their problems by actively engaging in the decision-making process of institutions (International Co-operative Alliance, 2013: 9). Especially young people with technological competencies are familiar with interactive communication and collaborative technological knowledge corresponding to cooperative values (International Co-operative Alliance, 2013: 10). Therefore, the new strategy should be adopted to draw young people to learn the cooperative identity and to create a collaborative community within the digitalized network society.

The second distinctive feature that constructs the cooperative identity is its sustainable business model. The cooperative model realizes the environmental and economic sustainability by harmonizing the different values of various stakeholders. Unlike the investor-owned company, cooperatives define themselves as people-centered businesses. The cooperative decision is not exclusively based on economic needs but also the social and environmental impact on the communities and stakeholders. Therefore, cooperatives do not seek to maximize one stakeholder's interests but to optimize the various stakeholders (International Co-operative Alliance, 2013: 14).

Sustainability provides cooperatives legitimacy and helps to understand the necessity of cooperatives. Cooperatives mainly contribute to economic sustainability. The member-owned enterprise model results in a safe financial model by pursuing the stakeholder value for sustainability. Members control their values and prioritize more human needs than the financial return. This member-ownership model provides the different business model focusing on other criteria beyond the financial performance and ultimately contribute to enhancing the diversity of business forms.

Several analyses prove that the goal of sustainability by far is achieved in the context of Korea's consumer cooperatives. The price strategy of consumer cooperatives reduces the price asymmetry of agricultural products, contributes to the price stability, and builds a sustainable food production system (see Chapter 4). In addition, collaborative SCM encourages multi-stakeholders to collaborate and ultimately enhance the whole supply chain performance (see Chapter 8).

However, sustainability is not only a concern of cooperatives but also of the various business organizations. Currently, social enterprises and investor-owned businesses also seek for corporate social responsibility. So, the challenges lie in sustainable practices of cooperative which might be different from other business forms. On the other hand, cooperatives have been highlighted by the distinctive feature of democratic control. The one-member-one-vote principle sustains its impact on member-owner participation so that the members may engage in improving the economic situation of their community.

In addition to two contributing themes that build a cooperative identity, it is required to improve the legal framework to sustain and ensure the growth of cooperatives. There has been a lack of awareness of the cooperative business model. Without the legislative support, this subsequently would have a negative effect on setting up the financial, legal and regulatory infrastructures favorable for cooperatives (International Co-operative Alliance, 2013: 26). However, it does not mean that the cooperatives need financial subsidies for the businesses. But it is necessary to support the social and economic activity of cooperatives. For example, the financing from member loans and access to non-members is prohibited for consumer cooperatives in Korea. It restrains business growth. Therefore, it is necessary to 'resist and fight for appropriate recognition and treatment' of supportive legal frameworks pursuing the development and sustainability of the distinctive business competency (International Co-operative Alliance, 2013: 26).

In this regard, there was a joint effort of Korea's consumer cooperatives revising the Consumer Cooperative Act in 2014. It represents the solidarity among consumer cooperatives to revise the Consumer Cooperative Act, which allows them to establish the federation to focus on their vision and sustainability. However, a legislative issue related to the access of capital remains a challenge for consumer cooperatives to secure financial resources for business operation. The current financial institutions should be improved for cooperative growth (see Chapter 5). Especially, the member loan should be legally admitted as a means of financing, ultimately helping cooperatives to get access to capital.

Capital as the fourth theme of the Blueprint indicates a requirement for cooperatives' establishment, development, and growth. Unlike the investor-owned companies financing their capital and the liabilities from bank or external investors, cooperatives have some distinctive features based on their cooperative identity. First, cooperative capital is different from investor-owned firm's share capital. Cooperative members are only guaranteed with the amount of share they invested. Second, the surplus of capital is controlled by members and the distribution in proportion depends on the membership (International Co-operative Alliance, 2013: 32). Thus, it is hard to attract investors' interest who make a priority in financial returns. However, it may be time to change. Since the financial crisis of subprime mortgage loan in 2008, the profit-maximizing model of the investor-owned business has shown its critical defects. Thus, the Blueprint suggests an ethical investment visioning the better world which denies the sole economic purpose of profit maximization. Moreover, the relevant financial system can secure reliable cooperative capital controlled by the members. It requires us to explore the various financial instruments to get access to capital 'but without compromising on member control' (International Co-operative Alliance, 2013: 33).

Based on the well-developed participation and sustainability with the favorable condition for the cooperative growth, the central theme of the Blueprint is to build and secure the cooperative identity (International Co-operative Alliance, 2013: 20). Cooperative identity has been supported by the cooperative seven principles and yet the interpretation varies by its cultural and societal context. While identity reflects the significance of cooperatives, cooperative messages imply outward brand identity projected by business and social activities of organizations such as marketing, education, and communication. Therefore, the message itself plays an important role to enhance the practical understanding of cooperatives for participation and sustainability.

In the context of Korean consumer cooperatives, the messages differ while cooperative identity has sustained with the common business and social practices. Four major Korean consumer cooperatives have developed their own brand identity based on their distinctive historical background and vision, although they seem to have identical features of the identities. iCOOP has its vision as 'ethical consumerism'; Hansalim as 'save all living things'; Dure as 'cooperation among our daily lives'; and lastly, Happycoop as 'women's rights and happiness' (see Chapter 6). Despite the diversity of brand identity, Korean consumer cooperatives in common aim to supply safe and organic agricultural products seeking cooperative values and principles. All in all, they pursue the people-centered and environmental-friendly economy.

As the Blueprint mainly focuses on emphasizing the cooperative identity, the following part discusses the future challenges with which Korean consumer cooperatives are faced. It indicates the three main areas to focus on and suggests the strategies to sustain the cooperative identities.

The evaluations based on the Blueprint suggest the business model of Korean consumer cooperatives shows strong performance in implementing the five themes. In terms of the issues with capital and relevant legal framework, they continue to look for new ways of financing capital (see Chapter 5). Although establishing a supportive legal framework for the capital issue is another challenge to deal with, this business model is contributing to the powerful claim about cooperatives. They have a way of doing better business, which brings a more effective balance to the global economy than the dominance of the investor-owned business model.

Could this model, then, be prospective and proceed favorably in the future of the cooperative sector? The environment of consumer cooperatives continues to change, which generates further challenges to overcome. These challenges may be something that nobody has ever thought of and we can imagine to some extent. When we can identify the challenges, we are able to formulate a strategy to prevent them. To do so, we need to acknowledge environmental changes that have a significant influence on the consumer cooperative sector, and then identify what is the forthcoming challenge.

Initiatives of Korean consumer cooperatives have been highly engaged with other social movements such as agriculture, environment, labor, women's rights and so on. Based on the cooperative values and principles being shared internationally, it was possible to position Korean consumer cooperatives so that they pursue and implement diversified social values through the business model, due to their historical background and practices. However, social and ethical values are becoming iconic terms among 21st-century businesses. Investor-owned corporations and business enterprises in the market have begun to participate in these practices under the name of corporate social responsibility. Furthermore, other forms of ethical corporations are increasing in number and developing within the social economy sector. The growing organic food market in Korea is evidence that demonstrates this trend (EU Gateway to Korea, 2018).

With the organic food market being mainstreamed and the social economy sector growing, cooperative values and ideas seem no longer a persuasive strategy to secure the originality of consumer cooperatives, because other forms of business also implement them in different manners. As the scope of practices is expanded with increasing participants, there are risks of value co-optation, dilution, and reputational risk (Doherty et al., 2012) – 'green-washing' of some corporate brands, for instance. Thus, it is more difficult for consumers to clarify authenticity in business practices. In this context, how can we distinguish consumer cooperatives from other forms of ethical businesses? How can we establish a cooperative identity?

Here we suggest the prior challenge for Korean consumer cooperatives is related to identity. According to the Blueprint, identity is the core values and principles of cooperation and the meaning of cooperatives upheld within the sector itself and its members. And it needs to be distinguished from the message, which is the way in which the identity of cooperatives is communicated and projected to the wider communities. Thus, we argue the consumer cooperative sector must pay attention and articulate their identity and project this through an authentic message that can resonate sustainably by itself.

Challenges and responses for Korea's consumer cooperatives

Cooperative identity is established through participation and sustainability. Among the indicative actions that the Blueprint is suggesting under the identity theme, Korean consumer cooperatives need to deal with three of them: participation of young people, cooperative education, and solidarity among cooperatives for sustainability.

First, we need more participation of young people. It is important to promote the identity of consumer cooperatives for them and to communicate with them. This can be achieved when understanding comes first as to the changing ways in which young people communicate and form relationships with each other through technology and social media. In that sense, we need more young professionals in management as well. Additionally, consumer cooperatives should engage in other social movements such as the environment, gender, and so on, to attract the broader public of potential members and young people, who might be interested in the sector that is ethical and participatory. It is necessary to let those potential members know what they value the most in their lives is also valued and promoted by consumer cooperatives. To secure their interest and make them engage voluntarily and sustainably, both unique and common features of consumer cooperatives should be shared with other social and ethical movements.

Second, the provision of cooperative education is important in cooperative sustainability. Education concerning cooperatives can be divided into two modes: cooperative ideas as a way of living and the cooperative business model. The former should be included within the curriculum at all stages of education, from nursery to higher education institutions. School lessons on cooperatives or social economy are conducted in some schools as an extracurricular program or in their exam-free term in Korea, but they are not mandatory. When students in school learn about the importance of cooperative values and history in everyday life, it would be possible to spread cooperative identity and messages to the widest range of people. The cooperative business model would be introduced at this stage as a means of implementing the values. Further research and development of theories and business models can be conducted in higher education institutions such as business schools in universities. Also, professional entities can adopt the consumer cooperative business model within their organizational structure and learn how to own, govern, manage, and evaluate their organizations in a cooperative way. Through building networks between practitioners, managers, and academicians, cooperative identity would be promoted more broadly and the cooperative sector could train future leaders who are acquainted with both theories and practices well enough to manage a cooperative.

Third, building solidarity among cooperatives is crucial in sustaining the cooperative sector. And the development of the consumer cooperative sector as a whole would lead to the sustainability of individual consumer cooperatives. Cooperatives with comparably larger resources and scale should support the newly emerging and small cooperatives. It is easy to think of only financial support when discussing this issue. However, we would like to emphasize social capital that consumer cooperatives possess a competitive advantage. By sharing social capital such as established networks, cooperatives can expand and grow. In doing so, cooperatives can enhance solidarity and establish a shared identity to collectively promote its identity and messages.

Consumer cooperatives are one of the new and growing cooperatives in Korea. Since the 1990s, turnover and memberships are dramatically increased, considering the Korean economy's performance of the last 20 years, with its relatively slow growth. Korea's consumer cooperatives have been overcoming the various kinds of challenges and becoming major food retailers. Nonetheless, consumer cooperatives will face new challenges such as aged population, sluggish economy, and emerging smart and intelligent technologies. We believe consumer cooperatives can respond properly and find business opportunities and cooperative values. This book provides not only descriptions of Korea's consumer cooperatives, but also suggestions for them.

References

Doherty, B., Davies, I., and Tranchell, S. (2012) 'Where Now for Fair Trade?' *Business History*, 55(2): 1–29.

EU Gateway to Korea (2018) *Market Opportunity Korea: Organic Food & Beverage*. www.eu-gateway.eu/sites/default/files/collections/document/file/market-opportunity-organic-food-beverage-korea_0.pdf (accessed 27 November 2018).

Fairbairn, B. (1994) *The Meaning of Rochdale: The Rochdale Pioneers and the Co-operative Principles*. Occasional Paper Series, No. 31778. Saskatoon, Canada: The University of Saskatchewan, Centre for the Study of Co-operatives.

Hilson, M. (2017) 'Co-operative History: Movements and Businesses.' In Hilson, M., Neunsinger, S., and Patmore, G. (eds.), *A Global History of Consumer Co-operation since 1850: Movements and Businesses*. Leiden, The Netherlands: Brill.

International Co-operative Alliance (2013) *Blueprint for a Cooperative Decade*. International Cooperative Alliance. https://ica.coop/sites/default/files/media_items/ICA%20Blueprint%20-%20Final%20version%20issued%207%20Feb%2013.pdf (accessed 27 July 2018).

Index

Printed in the United States
by Baker & Taylor Publisher Services